We Bought an Island

by Evelyn Atkins

For Babs, whose main entrance
made quite a splash

© Evelyn Atkins 1976

First published in the UK 1976
by George G Harrap & Co. Ltd.

Thirteenth edition published 1998 by:

Alexander Associates
Fowey, Cornwall PL23 1AR. UK.
e-mail: alex@nder.com www.nder.com

ISBN 1 899526 51 X

British Library Cataloguing in Publication Data. A catalogue record
for this book is available from the British Library.

Cover photo by Guy Newman - Apex Photo Agency, Exeter

Contents

Foreword to 13th edition

The author

It is thirty-four years since the adventures featured in this book took place: thirty-four years filled with further escapades some of which are recorded in the sequel *'Tales from our Cornish Island'*.

My sister Evelyn, the author, left this magic island for good in February 1997 after a very short illness, but she would be delighted to know that, by public demand, a further reprint of the first island saga has been made to delight another generation of island addicts.

Babs
25th August 1998.

The author
May 1995

Prologue

Island For Sale—off the Scottish coast—£30. It seemed the answer to a dream. A dream shared by many apparently, because although I wrote by return it was already sold.

What is this fascination about islands? Is it perhaps some half remembered magic of childhood that we take with us into adult life? Dreams of a treasure island where one can live an adventurous life in a glorious sunlit land teeming with cockatoos, luscious fruits and coconuts, bordering on a golden strand leading to an ever blue sparkling sea. Maybe it is just the hope that if only we could cut ourselves off from the mainstream of life all problems would be resolved, all frustrations would melt away.

Perhaps it was just as well that this particular island was already sold. At the time I was 19 and would have been hard put to find 30/– let alone £30.

It was a bitter disappointment nevertheless. I had just returned from a holiday in the Isle of Wight. To this day I can remember the breathtaking moment when I climbed to the top of Boniface Downs above Ventnor. Below, the blue sea shimmered in the sunshine; above, as far as the eye could see, the island was encircled by golden banks of cumulus clouds. It was as though the island had been crowned with a golden diadem. The magic of that moment was enhanced by the feeling of complete isolation, a sense of detachment from the world. As I stood entranced I wished a wish that one day I would come to live on an island, an island of my very own.

Decades were to pass. Decades during which holidays were spent visiting islands and climbing their cousins the mountains. The names chime like chords in one's memory: Skye, the Cuillins, Striding Edge, Ben Nevis, Wildspitz, the Wetterhorn, Zugspitzl. Wild, lonely places. Often one slept above the clouds.

Then came a holiday that triggered off a chain reaction of events that led eventually to the realisation of that youthful dream.

The holiday was spent in Wales. The first significant feature was that my sister Roselyn (Babs to the family) and I visited Caldy Island off the Pembrokeshire coast. During our early years Babs, the baby of the family, and I were in effect a generation apart. With the passage of time she had caught up, so to speak. Together we were enchanted by Caldy and the apparent idyll of island life. So much so that later, after our return from holiday, when St Catherine's Rock, a once fortified and now inhabited rock cum island, was up for sale, we contemplated buying it. We dropped the idea not because the price was beyond our means, which it was by many thousands of pounds, but because we said, dismissing the idea disdainfully, "It is too near the mainland." In fact it lies just off Tenby and one can cross by foot in a matter of minutes at low tide.

Now, nevertheless, there were two of us with incipient island fever.

The second event which we had no way of knowing would have such far-reaching effects on both our lives and careers was in the nature of a disaster. Slipping on a steep cliff I broke both the bones in my right leg. After a week in hospital in Wales and a further four months in plaster and still partly immobilised I returned to full time work, travelling each day in the rush hour from Surrey to a hectic job in the Staff Department of the Head Office of I.C.I. in London. Walking was still painful a year later. I never really picked up; a breakdown in general health resulted. Following a three month's illness I retired early.

It was during an additional eight month's sick leave I was generously given by I.C.I. that I made plans that, modest though they were, led by a chain of extraordinary chances to our becoming the owners of our very own island.

It is at this point therefore that the tale really begins.

Chapter 1
The scene is set

One advantage of early retirement is that one is still young enough to consider another career. One not so demanding, minus the stresses and strains of commuting to London and dealing with people and problems. Preferably one as far away from a telephone as possible.

Pottery perhaps. The thought of sitting in a world of one's own and throwing masterpieces to the rhythmic whirring of the wheel has a compulsive appeal. To fashion pots from clay with one's own hands, as had been done since time immemorial, would be creative, therapeutic and fulfilling. I couldn't wait. The fact that every activity makes demands and has its own frustrations and disappointments conveniently eluded me. I was all set to join the immortals—a Bernadette Leach at least.

Keeping to a well tried philosophy of last things first, a belief that if you keep your sights on the ends the ways and means would take care of themselves, I set about acquiring a kiln. After all you do not take up cooking unless you have an oven, so it seemed a reasonable idea. Nevertheless there was a certain amount of astonishment when I asked for an electric kiln as one of my retirement gifts from I.C.I. At the end of my sick leave I went up to the office to have it presented to me, in token, as it was too heavy for anyone to move except Pickford's. Everyone thought I looked much better in health. They also thought that I would need to be.

Next I booked in for a residential course in pottery with John Shelly, who at that time, with his wife Elizabeth, ran one week courses at their lovely 9th-century Manor home near Totnes in Devon.

Babs, like a star character in a play who performs off stage during the opening scenes then makes a telling and dramatic entrance later as the plot unfolds, on a lovely day in June deposited me by car at the gates of the manor.

There were eight others on the course all at different stages of ability. I was the only raw beginner. John Shelly, a tall intellectual, ascetic looking man had an impressive personality. Obviously believing in pushing people in off the deep end, he had us all throwing on the wheel at the very first lesson. I was absolutely terrified and clung to my lump of clay for dear life.

"Kick harder! Harder!" he commanded as he towered over me. I kicked as though I were in training for the World Cup at least. Desperately I hung on to the clay. It was my anchor. Without it I felt I might have taken a header through the nearest window as my leg zoomed back and forth.

"Harder! Harder! HARDER!" he ordered on the second and again on the third visit to my wheel. I kicked until my newly mended leg had no feeling left in it at all. I thought it had dropped off. Next time round he called over his wife Elizabeth, a sweet charming lady. "She's come to stick my leg on again," I thought hopefully.

"Look!" said John "A pot first time!" And there quite unbelievably, clasped between my hands was a pot.

"Most beginners' first efforts land on the ceiling," he said kindly. "You have very good hand control." Personally I thought then as I still think today that, apart from the sheer terror that made me cling on to the lump of clay, John Shelly hypnotised me into making it. I still have that pot and it has a place of honour as a symbol of the start of the adventures that led us to our island home.

Because of that first lucky effort John made me practise throwing until every bone in my body ached. I used to crawl into bed every night feeling like a penitent of old. My bedroom added to the illusion. Bare but for essential furniture, plain or white wood, the room with its stone walls whitewashed breathed the atmosphere of its 1000-year-old history. It could have been a monk's cell. A lucky monk nevertheless for the room was large and had a view of the mellowed courtyard and the beautiful Devon countryside beyond.

On the fourth day I tottered down to the pottery and climbed on to the wheel once more to force my aching limbs to set it in motion. I was thinking despondently "This must be what they meant by being broken on the wheel," when John loomed up from behind.

"You could become a very good potter," he smiled encouragingly. "When you leave here you must go to a good Art School as soon as possible. It will take years of hard practice, but you can do it."

That was enough for me. Forgetting my aching limbs and, conveniently, the years bit, I rushed off to the others on the course and announced that I intended to have a pottery of my own in the West Country, "residential, rather on these lines," I said grandly, waving my arms at the manor in general. That night over drinks in the local and not a bit put off by the fact that I had only four days of potting behind me they all clamoured to give me their addresses. "Just what is wanted," said one. "Somewhere one can holiday with the family and yet be able to pot." I still have those addresses but alas! they are hidden in a welter of papers stowed away somewhere on the island. Bill and Joyce Adams were two on the course with whom I became friendly. They have actually been here and previously were in on some of the dramatic moves. The others if they remember and ever read this will know that I did not break faith. Maybe one day they will get a surprise reminder from the past. Little did I think as we sipped our drinks that within 18 months I would indeed have my own pottery, in the West Country, on an island lived on by monks at the same time, give or take a hundred years, as John's Manor house first began its history. I did not tell John or Elizabeth of my plan. I felt sure he would not approve of running before one can kick. Nevertheless they have both been here twice and given their benediction. I shall always be grateful to John for his encouragement and his help in getting me over those first seemingly unsurmountable hurdles.

Back in Surrey I waited impatiently for the Autumn term at Epsom School of Art to begin. Meantime accidentally I found myself with a job— and a spare time occupation. Both these, too, were destined to have an effect on the future.

One day I went to the local post office-cum-stores to buy (a) a postage stamp (b) to enquire about joining the local National Savings Group so that I could continue with the regular savings scheme that we had *had* in the office and (c) to buy stamps to put on my National Insurance Card. All very straightforward it would appear. Certainly I found myself in possession of a postage stamp without any difficulty at all. It is said that some people are incident prone. Regrettably I fear that I come into this category. In no time at all the orderly queue in that tiny little post office/shop turned into a public meeting and it appeared to centre around me. In less time than it takes to recount the incident I found myself agreeing to be in charge of a Street National Savings Group. I was introduced to a Committee member who was present, the queue quietly reformed and I left an all but signed up member ready to "Fight in the Streets".

The case of the Insurance stamp became even more involved. For this apparently I had to apply at the Labour Exchange down in Epsom. Here I did my best to explain that I wished to buy an Insurance stamp. "No" I was told, they bought the stamp for me. "How kind!" I thought, handing over my card as requested. And that was that. So I thought. Later that day a pleasant female voice informed me on the telephone that she had found a job for me—typing and in charge of accounts. Panic gripped me. "Typing, accounts," I stuttered. "I am no good at all at those. In any case I don't actually want a job." Indeed I did not. For years I had been in charge of a large busy staff section, working early and late, chasing or being chased by people and papers, and baulked at every turn by the insistent and jangling demands of that torture, the telephone. In my spare time among many other activities I did freelance photography for the Publicity Department and as I did my own processing I frequently worked in my darkroom until 2 a.m. or 4 a.m. to meet the going to press deadline. I had had work. Now, fortified by eight months sick leave, all I wished to be was a potter. The helpful girl on the other end of the line explained; apparently I was now on their books and would be in receipt of Unemployment Benefit. Being offered a job was part of the arrangement.

"Well," I hedged, as she was being so kind and helpful, "perhaps a part time one then." That didn't count. It was arranged that I should go and see them again to sort it all out.

The next time I was in Epsom I called in. Proceeded by an elegant looking female trailing three dogs and smoking through a long cigarette holder I took my turn at the counter. "Sign please," said the clerk. Obediently I did so. "Nothing this week." he said and gave me £5. "But . . ." I started to say. "Come again next Wednesday," he added dealing once more with the elegant female who was still around. I looked at the notes. "Nothing!" I muttered to myself. I didn't understand at all.

The following Wednesday the same thing happened. I decided to resign. Babs was on school holiday and we intended to go off to the West country for a few weeks so the next Wednesday I stepped firmly up to the counter.

"I am leaving," I announced in a clear voice "I am going on holiday."

"Sign, please." said the clerk.

"For three weeks at least." I continued. The clerk looked up.

"Just leave us your holiday address."

"I haven't got one."

"Well send it as soon as you have in case anything turns up" he said, handing me a wad of notes. I felt trapped. I was a member of the Labour Exchange for life.

Soon after our return from holiday the girl with the helpful voice rang up again.

"We have just the job for you," she said "part-time receptionist at Halls, the coal merchants in Epsom."

"Ooh!" I quavered. "I don't think I would be any good at that. I don't know anything at all about nutty slack and that kind of thing. In any case receptionists are always young and blond, young anyway." "Well at least go and see them," she said. "It's *part time*" she urged. Thinking of all those wads of notes they had given me I could not but agree.

An appointment was made for me to see the Manager the next morning. To my great surprise I was engaged as part time receptionist starting on the following day.

The duties entailed taking orders from customers, dealing with their queries, and taking payment for their bills in person or by post. If the former, payment was made by cash or cheque. Everything had to be balanced up before the office closed for lunch and left, at 1 p.m. As customers came in right up to 1 o'clock waving money and bills, balancing up was quite a headache, especially as the chief clerk waited patiently at the door, keys a-dangling, to lock up before going to lunch. The telephonist whose switchboard was in a little cubby hole leading from the reception office was a particular comfort. Out of sight of the customers she would encourage me with sign language. I certainly needed moral support. For one thing I was not used to handling cash. My salary had always been paid into a bank account. Consequently I was in the habit of paying by cheque whenever possible. Cash transactions I did by weight—that is, I would hand over a note and if the weight of the change felt about right I accepted it. Now, as it was the firm's or other people's money, I had to be most meticulous. To count out change *and* keep up a pleasant conversation needed a dexterity of mind that eluded me. My friend in the cubby hole used to dissolve into laughter at my efforts to combine repartee and arithmetic. Mr Samuels, the General Manager who had engaged me, was very kind. A charming man, he did not criticize and there was never any unpleasantness if I were down on the day's takings nor if I made a bit for the firm.

Another problem was dealing with customer's complaints. If necessary the manager could always be called to deal with them, but it did seem that it was up to me to act as first line of defence.

One day a man strode in and brandished a shovelful of coal under my nose.

"Look at this!" he cried threateningly. "Do you call this coal? It won't burn at all, it only smoulders."

Not knowing what to do or say I gazed intently at the shovel hoping he would not throw the contents in my face. Suddenly I had an idea. "I expect your chimney needs sweeping," I said brightly. Wavering the shovel he stopped short, nonplussed.

"Perhaps you are right," he muttered. And to my intense relief he strode out again, shovel and all.

A few days later he was back. This time he brandished a bunch of flowers under my nose and presented them to me.

"You were right," he said, "my chimney *does* need sweeping." He called in several times after that to tell me the state of his chimney and he was always welcome because unwittingly he had provided me with a useful weapon in my verbal armoury. From then on "Your chimney needs sweeping" was my stock answer to similar complaints. It worked like a charm every time. In fact it had to be true for all the domestic fuels were tried out in the stove in my office. I soon came to know which burnt best, brightest or longest.

It was tricky though when customers complained of short weight. One man actually weighed every bit of coal from a one ton delivery on his bathroom scales, or so he said, to find that it was a few pounds short. It must have taken him a week at least. This gave me an idea.

"It has been belting with rain for weeks now," I reminded him. "The coal would get very wet standing out here in the yard when it was weighed. It would be dry and therefore lighter by the time you had finished weighing it." I called the manager nevertheless, as I always did for short weight complaints. This was dangerous ground and there could be far reaching repercussions.

My friend, the telephonist, said she enjoyed being on the same "watch" with me; she reckoned it was free entertainment.

I found coal fascinating. My knowledge was increased by a conducted tour of the heaps in the yard by the manager, some gleaming like black diamonds, and I just about knew the finer distinctions between Kitchen Nuts, Cobs, Derby Brights, Phurnacite and the rest when came enrolment day at the Art School.

With it came a severe set back to my plans. On the blackboard in the enrolment room were the fateful words "Pottery Classes FULL UP".

Going up to the desk I explained how important it was. Yes, they quite understood. Yes, they had heard of John Shelly, but it was out of the question: the classes were booked *for two years ahead*. The room was milling with frustrated would-be potters. A feeling of utter despair engulfed me and I was about to plough my way out through the shuntering throng when suddenly I saw at the bottom of the blackboard "Teachers' Class—1 vacancy." I fought my way back to the enrolment desk.

"Do you have to be a teacher of pottery to get into that?" I asked.

"No, you just have to be a teacher."

"Any kind of teacher?"

"Yes, any kind of teacher."

"In that case may I enrol my sister?"

"Certainly you can do that." And so I did.

Babs took it very philosophically.

"You must go," I implored, "and do your best to get me in when once you are there. It is my only hope."

She agreed although goodness knows she had little enough spare time to give to a wild goose chase. As Deputy Head of a new school which she and the Headmaster had started from scratch she had a lot on her plate. It was now a school of 1000 pupils and 46 staff. As well as being Headmistress to the girls she had recently had to take over the entire responsibility for the school due to the serious illness of the headmaster. Combining both jobs without a deputy to help *her* for two periods of six months was a great strain on her time and energy. As Careers teacher also she had organised a Careers Exhibition and for good measure a Leisure Exhibition that embraced the countryside for miles around. These exhibitions incidentally were so successful and had such appeal that one felt like going in for every activity on show. In fact it was through these exhibitions that I took up printing and bee-keeping, both of which have become rewarding parts of our lives on the island.

Any spare time Babs had was given to serving on N.U.T. Committees, organising parties and fetes in aid of Teachers' Charities, and taking part in or running the multifarious activities that take place outside of school hours. If at this particular point in time she was acting "off stage" as far as this tale is concerned she was certainly giving a marathon performance in her own particular sphere. Nevertheless she made a brief but telling entrance "on stage" by actually joining the pottery class as requested. Every week I eagerly awaited her return hoping that she had managed to enrol me. Each time she asked "Can my sister join too?" The answer was always the same: "No! it is impossible. The Office would never agree—the class is for teachers only." Each week my hopes were dashed to the ground once more. Then on the fourth week Babs burst in. "I've done it—you are in!" She had had an inspiration. "My sister *is* a teacher," she told Mrs O'Neill who was in charge of the class, "she teaches winemaking at an Evening Institute."

It was a fact. At one of Babs' private charity parties as an ardent winemaker I had apparently promised a friend of Babs, Ken Longley, who was Head of an Evening Institute that I would give a series of lectures in the coming term. I must have been an ardent wine imbiber too that evening because I had no recollection whatever of making any such promise and to this day the incident remains a complete blank. Nevertheless a letter officially appointing me arrived in due course from the Surrey Education Committee. Consequently every Tuesday evening for the last few weeks Babs had transported me plus all my equipment to this Evening Institute in darkest Surrey. There in the Domestic Science room I set up jars of wine, buckets, hydrometer and all the paraphernalia of this fascinating craft. With the room suitably labelled "WINEMAKING FOR BEGINNERS" I then proceeded to lecture and demonstrate to a class composed entirely of men. Bless them! they too must take their anonymous bow with Ken Longley for not only did they bring me samples of their but three week young wine to try, and much more acceptable I have to confess, the gift of a sack of pears, but their presence bestowed on me the accolade of teacher. For this magic word admitted me into what I had by now come to regard as the holy of holies—The Teachers' Pottery Class, Epsom School of Art.

Babs, her part done, thankfully returned to her busy life, merely adding the chore of ferrying me plus loads of clay and wet pots on Thursday nights to the Tuesday load-up to the winemaking class. How she fitted me in with all her commitments I shall never know. No doubt she felt she was performing a public service in keeping me quiet.

The pottery class was obviously full of geniuses. Gorgeous pots rose as if by magic under the hands of dedicated females. As they bowed as in supplication over their potter's wheels the air was filled with the sound of slapping clay and whirring wheels. At intervals one of these nun-like creatures arose, and, as with a votive offering in outstretched hands, would advance to the High Priestess bearing her work of art. This appeared to be a closed order, for very little speech accompanied the ritual. A few signs of benediction, an occasional censure, and the suppliant returned to her wheel elated or chastened accordingly.

Presently the High Priestess was joined by the High Priest and together they made a tour of the bowed figures, presumably to bestow a blessing, judging by the air of uplift that followed in their wake. Allow me to introduce Dennis O'Neill, Head of the Pottery School and his wife An, in charge of the teachers' class. Both were destined to play an important part in our saga. That was in the future. At the time I doubted whether I would ever become a member of that hallowed circle. With just one week's pottery to my credit and a mythical academic title I felt an uneasy novitiate; the possibility of excommunication a nagging fear. I need not have worried. Potters are a dedicated lot but ever ready to help and encourage their less expert members. Certainly I have always found this to be so. Soon under the patient guidance of An O'Neill I too was happily slapping clay and had the infinite satisfaction of again feeling wet clay rising under my hands on the spinning wheel to form that glorious bit of magic—a pot.

After a few weeks it seemed to me that the time was ripe to start looking for somewhere to have my own pottery. After all, I did have my own kiln. No matter that it takes years to become a fully fledged potter. With eyes firmly fixed on the distant goal it was not temerity or an exaggerated belief in my ability that made me think that I could overcome the intervening hurdles in record time; I merely ignored the possibility of their existence. Furthermore, life was beginning to crowd in on me again.

The National Savings Group which I had so impetuously joined was taking up an increasing amount of time. My "parish" was a street that consisted in the main of professional middle class members, who for reasons of health, age or young children, were housebound and consequently they welcomed the weekly visit. Their cares inevitably became my cares. In addition I had been asked to help canvass for new members in order to form more street groups. At first I felt it was a bit presumptuous to knock on people's doors and persuade them to save their money. One could not even say there was a war on and therefore it was a public duty. I had fallen into the National Savings Scheme so haphazardly on that eventual day when I had gone into the Post Office merely to buy a stamp that I was not sure exactly *why* we wanted people to save if they hadn't thought of doing it themselves. Soon, however, I had got caught up in the spirit of it all and felt it was a "GOOD THING".

It became quite a challenge to knock on a door and in that split second when it opened, try to get across the fact that you were not selling something or about to clonk the occupant on the head. It was surprising how well one was received and quite a number joined. At the end of each road we compared notes and there was keen rivalry as to who had bagged the most. Some of the houses we visited stood in their own grounds. I often wondered why their occupants whose husbands might have been stock-brokers and certainly were very well heeled did not tell us in no uncertain manner to save our time instead of telling them to save their money. They never did.

Quite suddenly I found myself a delegate at the National Conference at Folkestone and at the next meeting of the District committee was expected to stand up in the Council Chamber and make a report on it. How appropriate the saying "Great oaks from little acorns grow!"

The wine-making classes, photography, and for some inexplicable reason, a refresher course in German, wood-carving, and some political activity locally also made inroads on precious time and energy.

The main demands were, of course, those of the part-time receptionist's job. This frequently became full time as autumn colds and sickness hit the staff. Another pressing problem was that in spite of my somewhat unorthodox approach to customers I had, after a visit from one of the directors, been invited to become a member of the permanent staff, full time. Mr Samuels, the General Manager, had been so kind that it was going to be difficult to say "No".

There was yet another reason why it seemed propitious to move on. It can best be described as "The Case of the Bank Manager and the Book-shop." Like many other incidents it started in an unexceptional way. That is, someone came knocking on the door on behalf of Encyclopaedia Britannica. There was nothing extraordinary about that. Young men in their droves at this very moment must be knocking on doors all over the country on behalf of some encyclopaedia or other, but I am willing to wager that none of them has had such an unusual outcome as this one. Ever since Mother had helped me to buy a copy of Arthur Mee's Children's Encyclopaedia when I first earned the princely sum of £1.5s (£1.25) per week I had aspired to owning this one some day. With my retirement "lump sum" still burning in my pocket what better use for it than to spend a part on achieving this ambition?

"Come right in," I said. "I will have a set."

The young American was so astounded at making this lightning sale without any sales talk on his part at all that, deciding probably that I was not getting my money's worth in that direction, he gave me an excellent after sales service instead. Soon he got to calling in any time he was passing. He was mad keen on fast cars, and was always trading in the current car for an even longer, lower and faster one. He would call in and invite me for a spin in his latest model. It was quite terrifying. We would zoom off towards the Downs reaching 100 m.p.h. from scratch in about two seconds flat. While I clutched my stomach to stop it from shooting up like a lift and taking off for a solo flight of its own over the Downs, he would glance down at me and say proudly "Isn't she *great*?" To escape from this ordeal one evening I asked him in for a coffee instead. Babs was out as usual at one of her many activities. I told him of my plan for having a pottery in the West Country. "Gee!" he drawled, glancing round admiringly at our overspilling bookcases everywhere, "You don't want to waste your time on pottery. You should have a bookshop." He began to warm to the idea, and I got the impression that if it were not for fast cars he would have a bookshop himself. After that, every time he called he was full of this bookshop idea. "It would take a lot of capital," I objected, trying to fob him off. Because I liked buying books it did not necessarily follow that I would enjoy selling them. In fact the reverse would most likely be true, and I could imagine myself glaring at a customer I did not fancy wanting to buy one of my favourite books.

"No problem," he said, "I know a bank manager who will lend you the money. I will get him to call on you." With that he was off like a shot and made an appointment for the very next day.

Babs did not like the sound of any of this at all. So far she had not met my young American friend, and she thought that in some way I was being "got at". I did not quite see how. I had already bought his Encyclopaedia; he did not sell to shops and he was getting someone to lend *me* the money, not persuading me to invest any. It had not struck me as at all odd as I was used to these instant and unlikely "friendships". Only a few weeks earlier I had been to the Photographic Exhibition at Earl's Court. It was an enormous Exhibition with masses of people seething about. I no sooner entered and made a bee line for the Rolleiflex Stand in the Main Hall when a young fellow, a visitor also, spoke to me and in no time at all we were discussing the comparative merits of the different Rollei models. He then suggested that we spend the day together touring the exhibition. This we did all day until closing time. We had lunch together, each paying our own share, although he did at intervals buy me tea or coffee. He was starting a new job the next day down in Somerset, something to do with chemical research, and he was keen to discuss his prospects at what was really the beginning of his career. I told him too of my new "career" as a potter in the West Country and we had a really enjoyable day bound together by our common interest in photography. When closing time came we solemnly shook hands with each other he thanked me for my company and, wishing each other success in our respective enterprises, we went our separate ways. Ships that pass in the night. Why not?

Thinking it over however it did seem a little strange that a Bank Manager should call at one's home to offer a loan. Perhaps if you were a Paul Getty you might expect it, for it is a commonly held opinion and possibly a true one that you can always borrow money if you do not need it, but for those who have none there is no way. I was not a customer of this particular bank and it was in any case in a town several miles away from our nearest village or town, quite a journey for the Manager to make.

By the following lunchtime after leaving the office I was convinced I was being conned, or something even more sinister. The appointment was for 3 o'clock. By 2.30 I had arrived at the conclusion that the gang, for surely there would be an offshoot of the Mafia behind this, had, through their "front" man, decided that the bookcases would slide back to reveal hidden safes, as in the best thriller films. Anyone, they would reason, who bought an expensive set of encyclopaedias in ten seconds flat and proposed to buy property in the West Country to house a pottery must be well heeled. My young friend had cased the joint and now the gang headed by the supposed bank manager would muscle in for the crunch.

How would I defend myself? Not being a karate, kung-fu or even a judo expert the choice was limited. I no longer possessed a rifle from shooting days and was only accustomed to target shooting anyway. What about the old stand-by, pepper? You just threw it in the face of your assailants and while they were choking in agony dialled 999 and a Panda car would skid outside to a sickening halt and disgorge a posse of policemen who would whip the villains into handcuffs before they could sneeze "Atishoo." I fetched the pepper pot and put it in a handy place on the window sill by the front door. But wait! In this democratic country is it not illegal to carry an offensive weapon, or anything of a harmful nature even if it is intended only as a means of self protection? Better play safe and keep within the law. Regretfully I put the pepper pot back, then got it out again and cunningly put it in a strategic position on the sideboard. "It was the first thing that came to hand m'lud," I would state in court. "You showed great presence of mind," the Judge would say. "If more citizens acted like this there would soon be no criminals left."

As the villains were being led below to serve stiff prison sentences the doorbell rang and I nearly jumped out of my skin. I opened the door to find a very smart middle-aged gentleman standing there wearing a Homburg hat, gloves, and carrying a briefcase under his arm—just like a bank manager in fact. "A trick of the trade," I thought. After all, he would not come dressed like Bill Sykes complete with jemmy and a bag of tools.

"Come in!" I said cordially, trying to stop my voice from quavering. He came in and sat down. He was really most friendly and disarming. "Wait for it!" I said to myself. "This is just the softening up process." Nevertheless the conversation went along on most conventional lines. He took papers out of his case and asked me some ordinary straightforward questions. "Only a con trick after all then," I told myself, perhaps a little disappointed that I would not have the opportunity to thwart dastardly deeds with a simple culinary device. Yes, he would lend *me* the money, how much would I require? "It really depends," I hedged, "on the price of a suitable property", not daring to let on that I did not actually want a bookshop at all, but a pottery. "You will need stock, of course," he said, "and I feel that I really must give you a word of warning. You need a great deal of experience to know in advance what books will sell. Salesmen will try to convince you that what they are trying to sell will become bestsellers. If you haven't a nose for these things you could find yourself stocked up with a lot of white elephants. Unlike most other commodities you could find that you have a lot of capital tied up in something that will never sell."

"Well!" I thought, "this is the con trick to out-con all con tricks. Lull me into a false sense of security by giving me what was obviously very sound advice—just the sort of advice in fact that you would expect from a bank manager. The crunch will come later." Unexpectedly the crunch did not come by the time he rose to leave. "I will back you," he said handing me his card "but think very carefully and remember that though our young friend means well he is very impetuous. Ring me if you want any further advice and let me know when you find suitable premises."

After he had gone I glanced at his card. He was, it stated, the manager of a branch of one of the Big Five, in a very large town indeed. It sounded an important branch but if of course I rang the number I should get through to some back room of one of the gang. "I am really being set up," I muttered to myself. "I am now a sitting target, just ready for picking off." Just what I was being set up for I could not guess. Not the books obviously and my "lump sum" would hardly have the allure of a golden handshake of one of the Princes of Industry. It must be that my style of living gave the impression that I had hidden resources and I had been carefully cultivated until I was ripe for the picking. Well, I would soon find out. Tomorrow when the banks would be open again I would telephone, not the number on the card, but the one given in the telephone book for the branch shown on the card—if such a branch existed.

When Babs arrived home she was very worried indeed. "I don't see why. I haven't committed myself to anything," I explained, "and he actually offered to lend me money." She was much relieved to know that I intended ringing the bank and our suspicions being confirmed that would be the end of the matter.

The next day I looked up the Bank in the telephone directory and found surprisingly that the branch really existed, but I was astonished to find that the number was the same as that on the business card. I had intended enquiring about opening an account when I spoke to the real manager as I had to have some pretext for calling him; intending to move to the district or some such tale.

I called the number and asked to speak to the manager. When he came on the line he was the very same man who had called on me yesterday. Quickly I thought up some query arising out of our conversation of the day before. Courteously he advised me, again offered his help and we rang off. It was absolutely incredible. He really was a bank manager and the whole affair genuine. Babs could not believe it either and gave me a very strange look indeed. Later in our saga I dropped a note to him explaining that instead of a bookshop we had bought an island. I have often wondered what he thought about this and how we could find the money for an island if we needed a loan for a bookshop. Since that incident I have never really been able to look a pepper pot in the face either.

The next day my young American friend called round cock-a-hoop. "Now we must find you an estate agent," he enthused. "I think I know just the man—I will get him to call on you." "Don't do that," I said faintly, "get him to ring me instead." This he did and it was just as well for his journey to see me would have been even longer than the bank manager's. I explained that I was really looking for property that would serve as a

16

pottery or a bookshop, and in the West Country. He sounded rather puzzled, as well he might, but promised to keep a look out for me.

One way and another my affairs were getting involved, and the only way was to escape away from them. It was fortuitous therefore that Babs was just about to start her week's half term holiday, due the last week in October. During our holiday in Cornwall in August we had both decided that we would dearly love to live there. We had toured around looking at properties for sale. None was suitable. They were either crumbling mansions or derelict shells of cottages. Any dwelling that looked structurally sound and attractive turned out to be a guest house being sold as a "going concern" with a corresponding high price. Now on the first Sunday of her holiday we suddenly decided just half an hour before the post was due to go to write off to as many estate agents as possible in the time, asking for details of cottages for sale, preferably for £500 or under. With Sunday papers and guide books for reference, typewriter and carbons for speed, we managed to write to twenty-one and caught the post as the box was being emptied. I optimistically hoped that I could get time off so that we could leave Thursday lunchtime for a long weekend with as many replies as we had received by then.

Monday morning I presented myself to the chief clerk and asked if my part-time could be arranged so that I could leave at midday Thursday for the weekend. I would work full-time until then I obligingly added. He looked dubious and started to shake his head.

"It would still be part-time," I pointed out with what I considered was impeccable logic as though that was the crux of the matter. "More than part-time, in fact. I shall be working three and a half days and only having two off." This must have carried some weight because he agreed to see what he could arrange. Luckily no one was off sick and my colleagues were more than willing to help us with our venture and swop duties. And so it was arranged.

Chapter 2

Enter Fairy Godmother and Knight in Shining Armour

At 1 o'clock on Thursday the last day of October Babs called for me at the office and we set off armed with a sheaf of papers from estate agents and accompanied by our constant companion Toby, our smooth haired fox terrier. By 7 p.m. on a pitch dark night we had just left Plymouth and crossed the Tamar bridge into Cornwall when gale warnings were given out on the radio, as by the light of a torch I put all the agents' papers in geographical order. The nearest cottage for sale was in West Looe, just 19 miles into Cornwall. Presently we drew up outside the Copley Arms at Hessenford. Bathed in a glow of mellow light in the darkness the inn bade us welcome. We were actually halfway out of the car when one of those momentous decisions was made, trivial at the time but so far reaching in its repercussions that one can only think that Fate or some unseen power does take a hand in one's affairs.

"Let's go on to Looe and find somewhere there to stay," I remember saying. We both agreed it would be more fun to wake up by the sea. If we had stayed at Hessenford the chances are that we would have kept on the main road and by-passed Looe the next day, for there was only one cottage on our list in that part of Cornwall. The majority were much farther west and, as we only had Friday and Saturday before returning on Sunday, time was an important factor.

Neither of us had been to Looe before. We were enchanted with it the moment we crossed the bridge over the river from East to West Looe. Reflected in the river the harbour lights sparkled like a fairyland of stars on that wild October night. A "VACANCIES" sign hung invitingly from the window of The Harbour Moon, the first inn we came to along the quayside. Unfortunately as we walked up to the door the notice was taken down. We were not the only travellers abroad that night.

The proprietor was very sorry but no other rooms were open at that time of year. However he kindly telephoned a friend who appeared almost

18

at once, to lead us by car to his guest house. This was perched at the top of Shutta, a valley leading high up in the hills above Looe. The house could only be approached by driving the car for the last hundred yards in reverse. The lane was narrow and twisted upwards at a gradient of at least 1 in 4. To get into the driveway Babs had to shunt to and fro and finally reverse up and round an enormous tree—all this in the pitch dark. It was as well Babs is a good and experienced driver as it was some hazard to cope with at the end of a 240 miles journey. We realised now why our host had arrived so quickly down in Looe: he probably shot down from top to bottom in a nose dive. Our host, too, plays a small but important part and is in our *Dramatis Personae*, for as a baker's roundsman in the close season he not only knew the cottage we had come to view but the lady who owned it. What is more, he offered to take us there in the morning.

The cottage proved to be one of two nestling against each other in a minute cobbled courtyard. The walls were whitewashed and flowers were still in bloom round the horsebox-type door. It looked idyllic. The upper part of the door opened to reveal the top half of a lady to whom our host introduced us and then departed from us and from this tale.

"Are you sure it is not the one next door you want to see?" she asked. Astonished that both should be for sale, we mentally bought that one too, for we knew that we need go no further, need look at no more cottages. This was it. We had not actually crossed the threshold, indeed we had as yet only met the top half of the owner when we made this joint but so far unspoken decision. Whatever snags there were they would be overcome.

Oak-beamed with "two up and one down" it seemed a dream of a fisherman's cottage. It was to be sold freehold, and, for preference furnished. As the furniture included a new cooker, new radiogram, and money-consuming items like cutlery and china for hardly any difference in the asking price, we opted for that. For good measure the owner impulsively threw in her beautiful collection of horse brasses as she said she knew we would take good care of them. We did not quibble over the price, nor ask why she was leaving. In ten minutes flat from crossing the threshold we agreed to buy. We raced over to Hicks the estate agent in East Looe, paid the deposit and considered that as far as these things go the cottage was ours. We also asked him to arrange a survey in case any structural repairs were necessary, but in order not to hold up proceedings did not make it a condition of purchase. Armed with an order to view the adjoining cottage, which was empty, we dashed back to West Looe.

This cottage was completely bare; damp patches showed everywhere and plaster flaked off the walls and ceilings in huge chunks. This was a "one up, one down" although the landing had been partitioned off to make an extra minute bunk room. Downstairs the floor was stone-flagged; oak posts supported the oak-beamed ceiling; upstairs the walls of the bedroom were panelled. We looked at each other.

"Ideal for a pottery," we said simultaneously. "Downstairs for kiln and wheel, upstairs for storage."

So within hours of setting foot in Cornwall and just four months since John Shelly's pottery course we were virtually the owners of two cottages, one of which was the pottery designate. The prices were within our reach for this was 1963 before gazumping and rocketing prices, and the first cottage had been reduced in price as the summer season was well past. I still had most of the "lump sum" acquired on retirement and we also had a legacy from an aunt. This seemed an excellent use for both. By buying the two cottages we had, too, acquired the privacy of the courtyard. Looe is very hilly, rising steeply from both sides of the river. The "pottery" cottage, No 1 Bassett Court, is literally built into the side of a hill. The terrace and garden of our nearest neighbour is on a level with our roof, the sub-strata forming the fourth wall of our cottage. This accounts for the damp for which there seems to be no solution. Its unique placement has the advantage that Mr and Mrs Vague, who abutt us, keep a kindly eye on our roof and tell Babs when the guttering is blocked, a tile is missing, or the chimney needs repointing. This was to be all in the future. At that time all we knew was that we were on the level—a great advantage in hilly Looe—about 100 yards from the quayside and, rather temptingly, some fifteen yards from *The Jolly Sailor*, a sixteenth-century inn. Later we discovered that both cottages were reputed to be as old as *The Jolly Sailor*. There may be some truth in this for as I write they have both been designated as of historical and architectural interest. We had, of course, taken a chance in buying without a survey or search. The fact that both cottages were for sale independently might have signified that they were due for demolition or some other fate. Luckily for us it was pure coincidence that No 1 was also up for sale at the end of the summer letting season, for which purpose it had been used.

So jubilant were we with our rare good luck in finding our dream cottage, and unexpectedly doubling up on it, right at the start of our quest, that we were undeterred by the fact that during our to-ing and fro-ing between the cottages and the estate agent the river had overflowed its banks and swept up the street to within yards of *The Jolly Sailor* and perilously near our future abode. But for the railing there was no way of knowing where river and street ended or began. At the quayside cars and boats lay side by side in deep water. All the cottages leading to the river and those along the quayside had stormboards up, so the flooding appeared to be a usual occurrence. On the second trip back from the agent the road running alongside the river was completely submerged and we could only reach the cottage by nosing the car through flood water by narrow back streets. No one seemed to be worried by this state of affairs so we were prepared to do likewise. The cause of all this apparently was a combination of heavy rain from the south-west gale and an exceptionally high tide with which the manholes could not cope.

Mr Hicks introduced us to Mr Nancollas the surveyor and estate agent on our side of the river. It was he who was to make the survey as it would have been unethical for Mr Hicks, the agent responsible for the sale, to have done so himself. At the same time we arranged with Mr Nancollas for an application to be made for planning permission for No 1 Bassett Court for use as a pottery as soon as the purchasing formalities were completed. So, incredibly, within 24 hours of leaving, not only was our mission achieved but we had an embryo pottery thrown in for good measure.

Back at the Art School I diffidently told Mrs O'Neill about the cottage and that it was going to be a pottery. She did not turn a hair at what must have been a startling piece of news from her newest and rawest pupil. Indeed she was as delighted as we were when eventually unconditional planning permission was granted for the pottery. In fact both she and her husband did all they could to teach me as much as possible and introduced me to the mysteries of glaze making, a facet of pottery not usually covered in evening or part-time classes, and explained other technicalities that I would need to know, but which in my ignorance I did not even know existed.

Christmas, which followed only a few weeks later, saw us heading once more for Cornwall; this time to spend the holiday for the first time in our new little home, which we were now pleased to have bought already furnished. The kindly Mr Hicks had booked us into the Hannafore Point Hotel for lunch and dinner on Christmas Day, so, the festivities taken care of, we arrived at the cottage laden with gallons of paint, turps, paint brushes, cleaning materials and overalls as well as linen, Christmas presents, cards and a store of home-made wine.

It was exciting to wake up to the sound of strange footsteps on the cobbles and hear voices calling to each other in their rich Cornish tongue across Market Square. Our courtyard led into Market Square which is not square at all and is so tiny that occupants hold conversations with each other from opposite bedroom windows and doorways. Sometimes a fisherman's wife with perhaps a freshly baked long loaf under her arm, reminiscent of Brittany, would join in, so too would a fisherman on his way to his boat in the river. The whole effect was like a stage-set in a musical comedy or operetta, and as colourful. One would not be surprised if a window were to be flung open in one of the pink or whitewashed cottages perched on the hillside and a face appear to burst into an impassioned aria, or a chorus of fishermen were to march out of *The Jolly Sailor* singing excerpts from *The Pirates of Penzance*. It would not be surprising at all, for the Cornish are very musical and the Looe Singers or "Pennylanders" are a nationally known choir and have a delightfully sung record to their credit.

On one side of our courtyard entrance is a minute cottage owned by the West Looe Town Trust and used as a store. On the other side of the entrance is a mounting block from the days of horsemen, for the cottage flanking us on that side and facing Market Square used to be an inn called "The Cornish Arms". In the courtyard opposite our two cottages is a kind of outhouse which was used at that time as a milk store. In the centre of the Square is an hexagonal shaped structure once the market house, hence the name. It is at present a greengrocer's shop owned by another Shelley, Paul; he later was to become one of our *Dramatis Personae*.

We actually had a party in the cottage on Boxing Day. Our niece, whose folk on that side of the family are Devonians, and her husband who is also from Devon, although of Cornish extraction with the unmistakable Cornish name of Penhaligon, called over to spend the day with us from Devon where they were spending the holiday with her mother Molly, our brother Willie's widow. Even this meeting had a portent of our future. They brought with them another relative who was a young Cornish teacher and a friend of his, a girl from the Falkland Islands. We listened enthralled to tales of the Falkland Islands. Islands! islands! how we still dreamed of them. A short time after we were very thrilled when Molly herself came and spent a few days with us.

The rest of the holiday we spent painting in the "pottery" far into the night. After a long painting session we took Toby for a walk for a breath of fresh air, and were amazed to find the river over at East Looe ablaze with lights at 2 a.m. as the fishermen unloaded their catch from the luggers. In daytime with their many coloured sails they make a picturesque sight as they ride at anchor alongside the quay waiting for the tide to take them to sea once more.

Before returning to Surrey we contacted builders, a plumber and the Electricity Board, for there were improvements we wanted to make. We planned to have the plumbing altered in both cottages; washbasins with hot and cold installed in the bedrooms and in the inside lavatory in our No 2 residence. No 1, the "pottery", had an outside lavatory which for its purpose was enormous. As this actually adjoined the cottage we intended to convert it into a bathroom with washbasin and overhead heater. Both cottages were to have airing cupboards with immersion heaters for we had, after all, decided to keep the bedroom of the pottery as such instead of using it as a store for clay, glazes, etc. The reason was that our decorating and cleaning up of the panelling revealed it as an attractive room with possibilities. The "bunk room" would now be the store. We also arranged to have more light and power points.

Most of this was achieved by our next visit at the Easter holiday, but the decorating which we were doing ourselves went on interminably because the plaster pulled off in lumps with every brushful of paint like encrustments of stale cake icing. The whole lot really needed stripping back. Who knows what we should have found under the layers that had accumulated over the years, maybe centuries—perhaps a hidden room or some Elizabethan carvings? We had neither the time nor resources to find out, but eventually with the help of some size and five coats of paint the walls began to look quite presentable.

At Whitsun we were joined by two very good friends of ours, Bill and Marjorie Buck, both fervent do-it-yourselfers, who came down to lend us a hand and give us, we hoped, some of the benefit of their experience. Bill's forte was laying carpets and this he did with great expertise in spite of undulating walls and narrow twisting stairs.

The bedroom above the pottery in No 1, with its soft lighting, panelled walls and thick carpeting, now had an air of old-world luxury, invitingly comfortable for a weary potter to rest aching limbs. Perhaps it had become an incongruous appendage to a pottery, for many pottery workshops often resemble a bricklayer's yard. First it would need a bed. This was easier said than done for the window was too small and the stairs too narrow to allow the passage of a bed, double or even single. However, we reasoned, there must be a solution, for the room had always been used as a bedroom. In fact, we were under the impression that half the population of West Looe had been born in that room, for within weeks of our arrival we met at least three people who claimed that distinction for themselves or for an aunt or grandfather. An examination of the bed in No 2, which of course was part of the furniture that went with that cottage, solved the problem. This, although it was a traditional double bed with solid wooden framework, was hinged and so folded up for removal purposes. Later we were able to pick one up at one of the fortnightly auction sales held alternatively by Mr Hicks in East Looe and Nancollas and Lampshire in West Looe.

Bill, inspired by all the winemaking he had seen and sampled at our home, had recently taken it up himself. Between us we had quite a few bottles, so to celebrate the progress of the work in the cottages and the departure home of Bill and Marjorie the next day we decided on the spur of the moment around midnight to have a party. There was wine in plenty. In fact "Have wine—will travel," could have been one of our mottos for we rarely seemed to go on our journeys without some stowed away in our baggage. Food was the problem. We had nothing that would contribute to party "eats" except a packet of aspic. Chicken in aspic would be ideal if only we had the chicken.

This reminded us of an incident which Babs now related. When we first stayed at the cottage we needed to go out on a food shopping expedition. With our urban/rural background where shopping entailed a car ride into the nearest village or town or a 20 minute walk to the nearest row of shops we now proceeded to damp down the fire, dress up for all the rigours of weather that we might meet, put Toby on his lead, lock up and set forth with our shopping baskets for the forage. In five minutes flat, Babs told them, we were back, our baskets laden with food for the whole weekend.

"West Looe," we boasted "has every kind of shop you need literally within yards of the cottage, *and*, as each one is a family concern, you get personal service thrown in."

"Even your marvellous Toy Town couldn't produce chicken at this time of night though," said Marjorie, slightly aggrieved at the prospect of returning to the land of supermarkets and stores on the morrow.

"You never can tell," I said, accepting the challenge and with optimism raised to a high level by wine made from Surrey's best elderflowers I plunged out into the night. I do not know who was the most amazed when a few minutes later I returned with a leg of chicken in one hand and a cucumber and tomato in the other. By sheer luck a little café in the square had its lights on as its owner was still clearing up. In response to my frantic gesticulations at the window he opened the door to let me in, and probably relieved to find that he had no drama on his hands, kindly allowed me these items from his showcase. Was it mere coincidence, I wondered, that the name of the café was *The Witches' Cauldron*?

Marjorie was convinced that there was magic in the air and was more gloomy than ever at the thought of leaving tomorrow. There certainly was magic about as the next day was to prove.

In the morning, exhilarated by these events and not at all deflated by the fact that we did not actually have chicken in aspic as it did not set in time, I was up and out by 6 a.m. to take Toby for a walk. Although we had now stayed in the cottage several times we had been too busy decorating to explore and had not as yet seen the sea in spite of the fact that it had been our *raison d'être* for the coming to Looe in the first place. West Looe is separated from the sea front at Hannafore by steep downs and can be reached by a hilly motor road or an even hillier path, but this we did not know at that time.

On this fine May morning I proposed to cross the river and climb the Downs above East Looe to get a panoramic view of West Looe and, I hoped, at last a glimpse of the sea. East Looe Downs proved to be more built up on than I had anticipated and for some time we climbed and walked along made-up roads, rows of modern houses blocking out any view there might have been. At last a field appeared between the houses and, anxious to get grass under our feet and paws, we looked for a way in. To our delight there was a stile and a public footpath beyond. This led directly to an open meadow where sheep grazed and this sloped down the cliffs on the seaward side of East Looe.

Below at last was the sea shimmering in the early morning sunlight, but what riveted my gaze in spellbound astonishment was what I thought at first must be a mirage. There, beyond Hannafore, rising like a lost Atlantis out of the mist, was an island. Tender and green in the soft morning light it looked infinitely alluring as the mists melted in the rays of the rising sun. Enchanted, I took a photograph although I knew that no camera could capture the evanescent quality of the light or the magic of that moment of discovery.

I *had* to get back as quickly as I could to tell Babs. With Toby trotting by my side I hurtled down through farmland, and almost toppled over a fence down into Looe, then ran pausing for breath at intervals across the bridge down the quayside and so back to the cottage. Over breakfast we could talk of nothing else for we realised that as the island was only hidden from our sight by West Looe Downs, it was excitingly near.

Having waved Bill and Marjorie on their reluctant way Babs and I found the path that climbed up the side of the Downs above the harbour and, passing cottages and houses perched precariously above and below us, came down the other side to Hannafore. There, dominating the view, was the island. Less than a mile away it looked tantalisingly close yet with the sea between, elusively remote. Rising gracefully to the sky it looked like the tip of a submerged mountain. It seemed another world. Did anyone live there? We could see a cottage nestling in the woods below the slope of the summit and a house and a low building on the distant headland where the eastern tip ran down to the sea. How to set foot on the island? for that we must surely do. The answers to these questions would have to wait until we came down again in August for alas! we too had to return to Surrey the next day. But before that a most extraordinary incident occurred.

The next morning we had packed the car, Toby was on board and Babs at the wheel was ready for "off". I was just about to step in when a woman spoke to me. Now this in itself was not extraordinary. It seems to me sometimes that half the population is in the habit of stopping strangers and speaking to them, while others, probably the incident prone, seem to attract them like a magnet however many other people there may be around. It has happened to me so often that I once seriously considered carrying maps so that I could direct lost people. It would be quite impractical as I would need to hump a library around, for it happens in all manner of places; in crowded London streets, in open country, near home and in strange parts. If I were in darkest Africa I am sure someone would pop out from behind a tree and ask "Pleeze, ees thees the way for Istanbul?" or wherever. Something like this did happen once, only it was on Walton Heath about three miles from home. Babs and I were walking across the heath when someone *did* pop out from behind a bush and addressing me said "Have you seen Norah Rose?" Now by a strange coincidence I happened to know a Norah Rose who lived in a town about seven miles away from this quite lonely spot.

"Why, I saw her a week ago last Saturday in Sutton," I replied conversationally.

"I meant today," she exclaimed rather haughtily. "She is leading the field study group and I thought you were a member." Perhaps these strange coincidences are more common than I thought for when I related the incident to Norah Rose when I met her some months later, expecting her to be astonished, all she said was "Oh! yes, I *was* rather late."

Being picked on in a crowd is more puzzling. Once I was on a packed bus travelling to Victoria station in the rush hour. As we all clung on like flies someone leaned over the other passengers, tapped me on the shoulder and said "Will you please tell me when we get to the Army and Navy Stores?" At every stop I was asked if this were it so in the end I gave a running commentary, a sort of guided tour to the Army and Navy Stores. It was quite a relief when at last we reached it as I hadn't much breath left, squeezed as I was among all those passengers. This incident would not have been extraordinary if it were not for the fact that my persistent questioner was the conductor of the bus and this his first run on that route.

I have a theory about these encounters. Unable to follow the advice given by all those self-improvement books which promise success and a brilliant social future if only you train yourself to sally forth each day with a smile on your lips, radiating joy and confidence to all with whom you come in contact, I can only totter forth with furrowed brow and sheer misery oozing from every pore as I try to remember such things as where I put my Income Tax form or wonder what I can possibly get for the dog's dinner for a *change*. "Ah!" think these unhappy or lost strangers, "Here is someone even more miserable or worried than myself. Surely anyone with problems as big as *that* will lend an ear to mine or help me?"

Be that as it may, this person who stopped me in West Looe only wanted to have a chat. Babs, to whom this "instant friendship" was old routine, became restive and began to look rather meaningly at her wrist watch. That is until I poked my head in the window and said "This lady will clean our cottages for us." Babs was out of the car in a flash. One of our unresolved problems was that we needed someone to do just that and generally look after the cottages until we could come again for the summer holiday in two or three months' time.

As we showed her over the cottages our new found "treasure" made a

27

remark that literally made us stop dead in our tracks.

"I shall be glad of a nice little job like this," she said. "I have a room just a couple of minutes away from here in Hannafore Lane. You see I mostly live alone because my husband is the gardener over on the island and I won't stay there any more. It takes half an hour by boat and it is a terrible journey, sometimes the sea can be so rough. I just couldn't stand it any more."

We couldn't believe our ears and bombarded her with questions. "Who lives there? Is it possible to visit the island?" An elderly couple owned it, she told us. No, it was most unlikely that we would be allowed over there. They didn't like strangers visting them. "Elderly!" we both thought, not realising how comparative this term can be. "They won't want to live there for ever. They may even want to sell it, perhaps in the near future." Aloud we said, "Perhaps your husband would ask them if they would kindly allow us to land for a short time."

"I am sure they won't," she replied, "but I will get Arthur to come and see you when he is over here when you are hack in August."

Thrilled with our lucky contact we got back in the car to leave Looe at last. Or so we thought.

This is a modern fairy story and like all good ones it would not be complete without a fairy godmother and three wishes. Only the fairy godmother in this case was in the unlikely person of Alfy "Onions" (his surname was really Martin). Alfy was one of the people who had been born in our cottage. He was also porter to Mr Nancollas, the estate agent who had made the survey of the cottages. We had come to know Alfy through the fortnightly auction sales. In our absence back in Surrey Alfy had bid for us for items in which we were interested, up to a limit agreed between us based on his recommendations. He subsequently transported the purchases, including the folding bedstead, to the cottages. By reason of starting life in our No 1 cottage he took a special interest in us. As we passed the auction room on the quayside on our way home at last, Alfy appeared and stopped us to have a cheery word and wave us on our way. We chatted for a few minutes. Then as Babs put in the clutch we said "Well, Alfy, if we are going to spend a lot of time down here we shall need a boat, so you might look out for one for us, also we should like the milk store in the courtyard if that should become vacant, *and*" we added laughingly "if ever the island is for sale you might let us know." It had to be said laughingly for we had more or less gone over the top in buying the cottages and making the improvements. Nevertheless we had hopefully made our three wishes never thinking as we waved Alfy Martin goodbye that he would become our fairy godmother.

Back home we had other problems to crowd these thoughts out of our minds. The headmaster at Babs school, who twice had been seriously ill, died suddenly. Apart from the fact that they had started this new school together and he had become a personal friend, Babs had the additional worry of running the school solo again until a new headmaster was appointed. No sooner had he taken up his appointment than *he* was off sick for three months with heart trouble. Babs had little time to think of cottages in Cornwall or an island in the sun.

I had my problems, too, although they came into the nail biting category. First and foremost was how to resign from Hall's. Bab's summer holiday would be for six weeks and I simply had to be free by then to spend it with her, so that we could set up the pottery, enjoy the cottages after spending Christmas, Easter and Whitsun holidays working on them, and give Babs the break she so badly needed. Mr Samuels had been more than generous in letting me have extra leave at these holiday times so I did not want to let him down.

A minor problem that niggled me was that I had acquired a "banger" to get me down to Epsom and so relieve Babs of the chore of taxi-ing me to and fro from all the activities in which I had become involved. It was a beautifully kept car, almost vintage, and in perfect working order. Unfortunately I hadn't the courage to drive it. The husband of a colleague at Hall's came out with me two or three times a week to give me moral support. We drove over Epsom Downs where I executed three point turns, started on hills, drove in busy traffic and round the terrifying uncertainties of roundabouts. I had actually passed the test first time some years previously but having little driving experience since to my credit I insisted on having "L" plates up so that everyone would keep clear of me. My friend's husband laughed. He didn't know what I was worrying about. In fact he seemed to think that I was an accomplished driver and he certainly never appeared to mind putting his life in my hands. Nevertheless I just could not bring myself to go out in the car alone. So there it was in the drive, having to be moved every time Babs got the Wolseley out of the garage and still she had to pilot me around.

About this time too I felt despondent about my lack of progress at pottery. All the others in the class were turning out beautiful works of art, and they were so experienced. One was a teacher of pottery, another was on a diploma course and a third held her own exhibition annually. Mr O'Neill and his assistant Peter, who has since demonstrated pottery throwing on a T.V. show, were between them throwing a piece that was an impressive six feet high. It looked as though it had come straight out of *Chu Chin Chow*. I looked in despair at my own six inch efforts, higher than which I seemed unable to throw. To cheer me up Mrs O'Neill showed me how to throw multiple pots. To do this you threw maybe three pots of the same dimensions, you then knocked the bottoms out of two of them, mounted them one above the other and on the wheel somehow fused them into one tall pot. All went well until a stupid little accident held up further progress. One day at the office while rushing down the corridor to answer the phone two of my fingers got caught in the backward swing of the door. Hearing a scrunch I was not surprised when the fingers began to swell. To stop them stiffening up I used my hand as much as possible, throwing on the wheel that night until I could have fainted with fatigue. It was a wonder that I did not pass out for the next morning the hand was so swollen and painful that the chief clerk insisted on running me round to the hospital in the office car, and there it was discovered that one finger was fractured. Now with my hand in a splint and swathed in bandages I couldn't do any pottery at all.

Feeling generally rather despondent I resorted to that well tried panacea—a hair-do, with successful but totally unexpected results. Babs was to meet me outside the hairdresser's at the end of my appointment with Toby. When I came out, a very excited Babs awaited. With her was my old school friend "Tommy" whom I had not seen for a long time and the cause of the excitement was not the fact that they had run into each other.

"I've found someone to take on your job," cried Babs triumphantly. It could not have been a more fortuitous meeting. Tommy had recently given up a sweet shop she had been running to help eke out the family finances. Now that the children were educated and off their hands they had sold the shop, but Tommy soon found that she needed something to occupy her and was looking round for a job. Tommy had always, I remembered, been very good at maths at school, and with her experience of running the shop, balancing up and dealing with cash and customers would be child's play. Babs had once again come to my rescue.

The next day I went in to see Mr Samuels and told him that I wished to leave and why. "But" I added, "I have found a replacement, and, in fact, you will find that she is much better than I am." He was very charming about it. Everyone, I suppose, dreams of a cottage by the sea. Perhaps he did too. Anyway he was most sympathetic and agreeable about the arrangement, subject of course to interviewing Tommy, and he wished me well. Maybe he was just glad to see me go, but I don't think so. He was a nice man. Tommy got the job and apart from a merger and a different location she is still there to this day.

So, thanks to Babs, that problem was settled and for good measure Tommy's husband bought the banger from me.

There was an unexpected piece of good news at the Art School, too. To my great surprise and delight one of my multiple pots had been selected for the Art School exhibition. There it was among all the really gorgeous pieces by the experts. If anything was calculated to boost one's morale this was it. As soon as the bandages were off my hand I was back at the wheel and with renewed confidence, after being so long in the doldrums, my throwing began to improve at last. Another piece of news was even more unexpected and exciting. Mrs O'Neill came up to me at the wheel and said "The family and I are going to the New Forest for our holiday and Dennis has suggested that we come on to Cornwall for a couple of days to help and advise you with the setting up of your pottery—that is if you would like us to."

This was a wonderful offer especially as it would be in the nature of a busman's holiday for them. I couldn't help doing a dance of delight there and then in the pottery, and felt like throwing a lump of clay up at the ceiling. Babs was just as thrilled and, as the headmaster was now back in harness, we just could not wait for school to break up for the summer holiday and so be on our way once again to Cornwall for this momentous holiday. Just how momentous it was to be we could have no way of knowing.

Our good neighbour, Mr Oliver, advised us to leave our paint and brushes behind. "You will always find something to do if you take them, so have a real holiday for a change—you certainly deserve one." This was advice we were very willing to take, so that it was in carefree mood that we set forth sans paint, brushes, turps and rags, but loaded up instead with relaxation impedimenta of books, radios, T.V., cameras, sketch pads and the inevitable bottles of wine plus, of course, our good companion Toby.

We were settling into the cottage on a wet and windy day, which is not uncommon in early August, when Mrs Scott called to see us to report on

31

the cottages which she had kept in excellent order. She told us that her husband Arthur was over from the island on his day off and would shortly be in to see us. Not long after this there was a knock on our "horse-box" door. The wind howled as we opened it and there, framed in the doorway, stood a figure clad in oilskins, sou'wester and sea boots. Accustomed as we were to males immaculately dressed in gents natty suiting or stylish tweeds this apparition looked to us like someone straight out of an Agatha Christie thriller. As he stood palefaced and silent in the oak-beamed room with rain dripping from his oilskins on to the stone-flagged floor we both felt, knowing that he had just sailed over from the island, that this was a most dramatic moment and he the most romantic of figures. Alas! our dreams and illusions were shattered when he spoke. He had had a wet, rough and uncomfortable journey, and sadly for us there was no hope of our visiting the island. "The Whitehouses" he said, "just do not like strangers setting foot on the island." He promised, however, to ask at a suitable moment, but he held out no hope at all. We were not too downcast. The fact that the gardener's wife worked for us and the gardener himself had been to visit us brought the island sharply into focus. Only one more step and we might indeed set foot on the island. "Our chance will come" we told each other optimistically. That chance was to come, but in a most unexpected way.

The weather soon cleared and was brilliantly sunny. Looe in season was very different from the rest of the year. We had only seen it in late October, Christmas, and Easter and the season had scarcely begun when we were last down at Whitsun. Now the streets and quaysides were teeming with summer visitors. Hired boats plied between the river and the open sea against the background of the many coloured sails of the luggers riding at anchor along the harbour walls. This, the fishing fleet, would be sailing with the tide, their owners alternating fishing in the summer months with taking private parties on sharking trips out beyond Eddystone lighthouse, twelve miles away. Holiday fishermen and small boys cast their lines hopefully over the harbour walls, sometimes entangling with passing craft. Gulls swooped overhead on the look-out for tit-bits, their wings flashing against the blue sky and the backcloth of the pink and white-washed cottages perched on the hills that rise steeply on either side of the river; their haunting cries pierced the air above the chugging of the engines and the creamy voices of the boatmen calling across the water to muster customers down the harbour steps into the boats.

One of these boatmen, to our surprise, turned out to be Alfy Martin, resplendent in fisherman's jersey, cap and sea boots, following his summer occupation of hiring out "doodle-bugs"—the local nickname for small self-drive motor boats. He appeared far too busy to be interrupted, involved as he was in dealing with the queues of eager would-be motor boaters.

We explored Looe, but could not see the island. East Looe has a narrow sea front tucked between Banjo pier—a stone jetty extending beyond the harbour walls—and the cliffs, but any view of Looe Island, as we discovered it is called locally, is obscured by Hannafore Point which juts out into the sea on the West Looe side of the river mouth. In fact many visitors to East Looe spend their entire holiday ignorant of the existence of an island "just around the corner."

We spent the first part of the holiday exploring the beaches of Cornwall. For some years, long before the popular pastime it is now, we had been avid collectors of gemstones. Cornwall is a happy hunting ground for gemmologists and on previous holidays we had spent many absorbing hours searching for semi-precious stones on the rocky beaches. A Cornish lady, whose profession it was, had in the past given us much valuable advice and guidance, and we were now able to identify carnelians, banded, moss and fortification agate, rose quartz, amethyst quartz and topaz. Our collection now began to grow impressively. Bucketfuls of "treasure" appeared in the courtyard to be sorted out at leisure. "Perhaps," we thought wistfully, as we dropped them into pans of seawater to bring back the colour and brilliance that had attracted us to pick them up, "Perhaps one day we shall find enough valuable ones to buy 'that island' if ever it is for sale." Maybe we rubbed a magic gem as we fingered through the myriad coloured pebbles. Maybe it was just chance or destiny taking a hand once more in our affairs; whatever the reason, something decided us on one particular day and no other to have a word with Alfy. We had seen him many times dealing with the seemingly never ending queue of customers for his boats. This particular day was after we had been on holiday for about two weeks, for having the cottage meant that we could spend the whole of the school holiday in Looe. Alfy was as busy as ever, but I remember saying "We really must speak to him—he may think that we are ignoring him." Rather diffidently we edged our way up to him.

"Hallo! Alfy," we said. "We don't suppose you will remember us, but you helped us with our furniture back in the winter." Quickly he detached himself from the crowd.

"Of course I do," he said, "and I have been on the lookout for you today—*The Island is for sale!*"

As though someone had fired a gun and without saying a single word to each other we raced to the ferry, shot across the river and up the stairs to the office of Nancollas & Lampshire. We paused for breath only to find that Mr Nancollas was out. His secretary made an appointment for us for 2 o'clock that afternoon. As soon as the doors were open after the lunch hour we were there.

"I am so sorry I was out when you called," said Mr Nancollas, "but I was over on the Island taking it on our books."

"That is exactly what we have come to see you about" we said to a very surprised Mr Nancollas, marvelling to ourselves that we should have picked on this very day of all days to greet Alfy Martin.

A few minutes later we left with an order to view—there were no details available yet, of course, just a hurriedly typed slip of paper. The asking price we noted was £22,000. It might just as well have been £2,000,000 or £2,000, for all were at that time equally beyond our reach. We did think, however, that as islands go it seemed a reasonable amount. This, being 1964, was before the days of roaring inflation, but it was still a sizeable amount for anyone to find—a fortune to us.

Our main reaction was that we had this magic slip of paper, a passport to "our island". The future would take care of itself. We did not even discuss ways and means—we dare not.

It was too late to go over that day. In any case Mr Nancollas wanted to warn the owners that we were coming if he could get a message to them. Apparently he was not able to do so for the next morning, as Alfy was fixing up with a boatman to take us over, a boat came into the harbour mouth and a couple stepped ashore. A helpful boatman ran after them and introduced us, for they were the owners of the island, Mr and Mrs Whitehouse. Rather startled that they had prospective buyers before details had been circulated they nevertheless cancelled their shore trip and took us straight back to the island.

Although we were so excited at the prospect of viewing the island we were sorry to hear the reason for the sale. Mr Whitehouse had contracted a serious illness and his doctor had insisted that he should remove to the mainland where medical aid would be immediately available. They were a charming couple and obviously loved the island. They showed us the main dwelling, "Island House" with its farmhouse kitchen, stoneflagged and oak-beamed; the lounge with its huge windows facing south and west with magnificent views of the sea; the two cottages and the many out-houses. We climbed the hill some 150 feet high and down through the woods to the tractor shed. We were shown the cliff walks, the beaches, the bridge to the "Little Island" and the daffodil fields were fifteen different varieties grew. These start to bloom at Christmas time and were sent to Covent Garden by the hundredweight.

But of all the fascinating things we saw the one that rivetted our atten-tion was the generator building. The front part of this housed a diesel en-gine for generating A.C. electricity. A doorway led to another room at the rear. This was about forty feet by twenty feet, one wall of which was lined with a row of large glass accumulators. Concrete blocks supported heavy wooden beams which ran the entire length of the room, and, apart from gangways, filled all available floor space. Mr Whitehouse explained that the previous owner, Major General Rawlings, a "D" Day Commander in the second world war, had retired to the island, and with the assistance of two families had run it as a market garden and daffodil farm, the mild climate, which was similar to the Scillies, making it ideal for producing early crops. In his day the electrical system had been D.C. and had been stored in accumulators in this room—hence the concrete blocks and beams for supporting them. Tragically the General died suddenly while on his way to Plymouth by train. Mr Whitehouse explained that when they came here to retire they brought their gardener and wife with them. Although they continued to cultivate the daffodils as they were in situ, they had no intention of carrying on with full scale market gardening and so did not need the powerful electrical storage plant. He had therefore dismantled it and installed the small but efficient Lister Start-O-Matic A.C. Generator, merely retaining one row of batteries for the initial starting up of the en-gine—or so we understood. All this was very interesting but technically beyond us. What held us spellbound was that this room, full though it was with concrete blocks and wooden beams, was simply crying out to be con-verted into a pottery.

Entranced, we walked back down the path to the beach where the boat-man was waiting to take us back to Looe. The island was idyllic, an abso-lute paradise. "But it is a dream, an impossible dream," we thought as we turned to shake hands with Mr Whitehouse. The next moment we really thought that we were dreaming.

"I suppose," he said hesitantly "you haven't had time to think about it. You will need to talk it over, of course."

"We certainly would like to buy it," we both exclaimed together, "indeed we *would.*"

"I would like you to have it and if you are seriously interested I will drop the price by £2,000 and let you have half the purchase price on a private mortgage of 6½%."

We stared at him in amazement. Did he really say that? Suddenly the impossible seemed within the realms of possibility.

"In that case," we both said at once, without any hesitation, not even turning to each other for confirmation, "we will have it."

Dazed, we returned to the mainland to think out ways and means of raising the other half of the money. Luckily we had a house that we could sell and I had some shares acquired in more affluent earning days when I had indulged in the giddy excitement of dabbling on the stock exchange. Babs had a legacy; then we had the cottages. With sessions of "Monopoly" in mind we thought that if necessary we could mortgage those. One way or another we might be able to raise the money—we *would* do it!

The next day the O'Neills were due to come down to advise about the pottery in No 1 cottage. Whatever would they think now? Having sat them in a circle in the little sitting room of No 2 we both stood behind the counter arrangement that served as a partition between the sitting room and the slip of a kitchenette, and handed them cups of tea, dispensing them as though we were serving in a cafeteria.

"We have an announcement to make," we said. "There has been a change of plan."

They all looked up expectantly wondering perhaps if the pottery project had been ditched and their journey had been for nothing.

"We are buying an island," we announced," and the pottery is to be there instead."

They were dumbfounded and then as excited as we were.

"Nothing has been settled yet," we told them," and we haven't actually found the ways and means, because the idea is as new as yesterday."

Instantly Dennis said that they would extend their holiday so that they could come over and see the island. We managed to get a message over to the Whitehouses and the following day a boatload of us sailed out of the harbour and disembarked on the island beach. As we all trooped up the path An O'Neill turned to us and with wonder in her eyes said "I shouldn't hesitate—you *must* have it."

Before Dennis, An and family departed the following day they came to see us again in the cottage. Over coffee Dennis said that he had thought up a few ideas that might be useful. He would, if we wished, lend us two of his fulltime diploma course pottery students for two or three months. They would convert the spare generator room into a pottery. This would not only be a help to us but would give them valuable experience in setting up a pottery as they were near the end of what was at that time a seven year course. They would be experienced potters and could do potting for me as well. We were delighted with this idea as quite a bit of structural alteration would have to be made before the generator room could be used as a pottery. Hefty young men would be invaluable in getting rid of the builtin concrete blocks and knocking a hole in the outside wall to make a door, and windows. Dennis also offered to come with his family the following summer to help with pioneering generally in any way that was needed. He thought that Peter Steele, his assistant—his co-thrower on the six foot pot— and his family would also be willing to come and do the same. They would all bring their own tents and be self sufficient and no burden to us. These were wonderful offers and seemed to set the seal on the venture. Getting down to practical details had the effect of dispelling the dream-like aura that surrounded the whole enterprise.

After they left we faced a few other practical details, details that were more in the nature of obstacles to be overcome. First and foremost was the question of raising the money, but this we dismissed rather casually. £10,000 is a large amount in anybody's money but in 1964, before inflation took the bit between its teeth, it was a fortune. And that would only be the beginning—there would be solicitors' fees for both selling our house and for buying the island; repayment of an existing mortgage, and removal charges, to name but a few. In fact the sum that was eventually required exceeded the basic amount by about 40%–50%. This problem we were convinced would be resolved. Surely we were meant to have the island, we said to each other, as we reflected in wonderment on the fact that every move we had made during the past year and any chance encounter had led us to what seemed this moment of destiny. Somehow or other the money would be forthcoming—nothing could diminish our buoyant optimism about this.

The one fact that did bring us up with a jolt was the question of Babs' career, for it suddenly hit us in the face like a slap of cold water that she would have to give up her job. In the fever of excitement at the enchanting prospect of owning an island we had overlooked this vital point. Nevertheless we airily brushed aside this problem, too; she would get a teaching post in Cornwall. It would mean giving up her senior position, which was considered a plum job in Surrey, and a big drop in salary, but some sacrifice had to be made, we told each other, in exchange for a passport to paradise. If we had known at the time how few teaching posts were then available in Cornwall and how rare the movement of personnel compared with the general post that went on in London and the Home Counties we would have been appalled at our optimism. However we remained completely sanguine—we were in a dream world and as each obstacle arose in our minds we just talked it out of existence.

After a time reaction set in. These big and very real problems caused us no concern at all. What did begin to worry us and nag us out of sleep was the ever growing fear that some rich person would come along and outbid us; our belief that the island was meant for us did falter at this possibility. There were certain preliminary formalities to be gone through before we could return to Surrey and wind up our affairs there, and these took time. So in theory we had time on our hands to enjoy at leisure; in practice we just did not know how to contain ourselves. We endured many agonising moments and almost gave up eating for the rest of our stay. There was the day, for instance, when we sat above the rocks at Hannafore, and just gazed across at the island. To our consternation we saw a man standing on the cliffs at the eastern tip of the island. He did not move and to our despairing minds he appeared to be surveying the scene of his future possession. "He'll outbid us!" we both exclaimed hopelessly. Another ten minutes went by and still he remained motionless. "He is absolutely gone on the place," we muttered. Despondently we fetched the binoculars from the car hoping that by magnifying his image we could will him away the more easily. To our intense relief we found that the object of our fear and despair was nothing more than a post. Later we were to discover that it was the tabernacle for seating the flagstaff.

More ominous was the day Alfy Martin detached himself from his queue of holidaymakers to speak to us.

"Mr Nancollas has taken a man out to the Island," he informed us. "I think it may be another client." His face was sympathetic and troubled, for as our sponsor, so to speak, he was as perturbed as we were. To keep our nerves from snapping we went for a run in the car along the coast to

Downderry. This was a mistake, for looking westward there was a magnificent view of the island. From this part of the coast it appeared to be much farther out to sea and in the soft light of the westering sun it looked infinitely alluring. We could not bear to look nor endure the suspense any longer, so we drove dejectedly back to Looe. Alfy's crowds had melted away by this time and he was waiting for us.

"It's all right," he said, smiling cheerily, "that was Mr Whitehouse's solicitor."

Our fears were not unfounded, however. This was before the days of gazumping and so far nothing had been signed and no deposit had been paid. Therefore when Mr Nancollas told us that some famous West End actors were after the island and offering far more than the original asking price we were in utter despair. The next day we saw Mr Whitehouse on the quayside. He came towards us. This would be it—the coup de grace; our hopes dashed to the ground and with one blow the end of a dream. After the greetings he looked intently at us.

"Some actors want the island," he said. So it was true and we knew that we couldn't compete. "I know that I cannot ask you legally, but I would like some reassurance that you will not resell to them."

"Resell!" we exclaimed, almost shouting in relief, "Resell! Of *course*, we won't resell, we are only interested in buying." There was no reason, of course why Mr Whitehouse should not sell to them himself at the higher price, but, as Mr Nancollas told us later, he really wanted us to have the island. Nor could he be certain that as soon as everything was signed and sealed we would not, without even taking possession, resell to the actors and make a handsome profit. In fact the ink was scarcely dry when we did eventually sign before we had an offer of £33,000, and could, just by the stroke of a pen, have made what would have been to us, a small fortune. In letting us have the island at a reduced price Mr Whitehouse was taking a very real chance. It was fortunate for us that loving the island as both he and his wife did that they liked our idea of setting up a pottery there, for we had discussed our project with them. On the other hand it must be said that later, when we had become well established, local opinion had it that it was also fortunate for the island that we bought it. Had it been on the open market it is certain that other offers than that made by the actors would have been made. The Scillies apart, an inhabitable island off the coast of Cornwall is a rarity. This one, said to be the largest, is outstandingly beautiful and unspoilt, and would have been ripe for exploitation and commercialism. It was considered a danger that it might fall into the hands of a developer and be turned into a holiday camp.

These conjectures and fears apart it was apparent from this conversation on the quayside that the negotiations were still taking place as arranged. So dear Mr Whitehouse who, sadly, died not many months after returning to the mainland to live, became our knight in shining armour who made it possible for us to take the chance of a lifetime and make that childhood dream come true.

Our friendly bank manager in Surrey advanced the £2,000 needed for the deposit so, the preliminaries over, there was no reason why we should not return home to work out the manifold problems of uprooting ourselves and finding the rest of the money. For some inexplicable reason we decided to stay on and finish the rest of the holiday as we originally intended. To be precise we, as usual, talked ourselves into staying, although there was nothing further we could do for the time being to expedite the negotiations. Firstly, we could not actually take possession until Christmas because Babs had to give a term's notice. Secondly, we really wanted to keep our eye on the island until the last possible moment because nothing would be absolutely certain until contracts were exchanged. We must be on hand as long as possible, we told ourselves, in case there were a hitch of any kind. Thirdly, and the most important reason, although we did not even admit it to ourselves, was that we wanted to put off the moment when we should have to face harsh reality as long as we possibly could.

So far everything had been done by mirrors; our friends, if they knew, would say that we were living in cloud cuckoo land. There was no escaping the fact that as soon as we returned home we would come down to earth with a bump. When Babs resigned she would be cutting off her career for an uncertain future. Then there was the matter of selling our home and giving up our whole way of life and friends to live on a remote island where we should be the only inhabitants. The only inhabitants? this raised a doubt which we pushed firmly down every time it raised its niggling head. The doubt was, not that we should be the only inhabitants, but that there might be only one inhabitant—me, for Babs would surely have to live on the mainland during term time. As Cornwall is some eighty miles in length the teaching post she obtained might possibly be too far away for her to use the cottage in Looe either, except at week-ends and holidays. Then there was the biggest problem of all—finding the money. This, the hardest nut of all to crack, concerned us the least. In fact we quite enjoyed thinking up ways of getting it. Many, one could almost say, happy hours were spent during the last fortnight of the holiday discussing schemes, so much so that we practically formed our own Government "Ways and means" Department. Not that we were idle in other directions. Life on the island conjured up all sorts of fascinating occupations and pastimes. One which appealed to us especially was astronomy and where better for a grandstand view of the stars? We therefore were delighted, when on a foraging expedition in the Barbican at Plymouth, to pick up a highly efficient Japanese telescope that had a magnification of twenty-five times and zoomed up to eighty times. It cost £12 and seemed a very reasonable price to pay after spending our time thinking in thousands of pounds.

Chapter 3

Exits and entrances

In early September we at last returned to Surrey to set the wheels in motion at that end, having left all the legal arrangements to do with the transaction in the hands of Mr Browning, the solicitor who had acted for us over the purchase of the cottages. Mr Nancollas was to keep an eye on our affairs in other directions. As Chairman of the Council, equivalent to Mayor, he had an official interest in the future of the island as well as the professional one of selling it to us. He took a particular interest in helping us, for selling an island is not an everyday occurrence in the life of an estate agent, and there were many details to be sorted out that were difficult for us to attend to from a distance of 240 miles.

When the news broke our friends were horrified.

"Whatever will you do, leaving all your friends?" asked Cyril and Doreen, two very good friends of ours. Cyril, a teacher by profession but an expert handyman, had always kept a kindly eye on us and helped us with painting, decorating and in the garden. He was quite concerned. How would we manage?

"Who will run our parties?" wailed Doreen, his wife. This was no idle question. These were the parties that Babs organised, ostensibly for various charities to do with the local N.U.T. They were highly successful and raised nice little sums for the funds concerned. Their popularity, however, was due to the fact that they provided social occasions for our friends in novel and enjoyable circumstances. Babs has an undeniable flair for organisation, and these parties were planned with as much overall vision plus attention to detail as would have been given to a vast military operation.

They went something like this. A theme was chosen and guests were required to come dressed accordingly; they also brought appropriate food and drink—although Babs usually provided the bulk of the "eats" as this gave her scope for artistic ability. When, for instance, the theme was "Cornish" this was loosely interpreted as anything to do with the sea. The Sunday before the party we felt it was essential to make a 100-mile journey by car to the coast and back merely to collect seaweed to use as part of the decor. Willing helpers festooned our sunlounge with cricket nets on which were hung these strands of seaweed, shells, corks and anything else that had a remotely maritime connection. An artistic friend, Joan Passingham, then erected a painted backcloth to represent a Cornish harbour, and to this she, with considerable ingenuity, had given a remarkable illusion of 3D. It appeared to reach on to the dining table which Babs had cleverly covered to give a startlingly vivid impression of the sea. Amid the waves rode all manner of craft, from sailing dinghies to ocean-going liners. They were all edible, as were the pebbles on the beach. Apart from concocting these delicacies Babs temptingly arranged prawns and shrimps in scallop shells which nestled beside the harbour walls. Seagulls and miniature lobster pots completed the scene and in the light of the storm lanterns, which were the only source of illumination, the general effect was surprisingly effective. And this was only the sun lounge, for the whole house was given over to these parties and in the garden, too, for those held in the summer. At this particular one Joan Passingham, after she had set up her harbour scene, took up residence in the attic where she invited guests to climb the loft ladder at sixpence a time to see the "water otter", this being a kettle nestling in a bed of straw. We had fortune telling, too, but it was not foretold, nor did we guess, that this particular party had a prophetic significance, for it was dreamed up before our thoughts turned westward; at least, our thoughts of removing there lock, stock and barrel.

Friends of all age groups attended these parties, and cars lined the road in both directions as far as the eye could see. Neighbours would have been startled to see pirates, gypsies, Spanish matadors and Chinese Mandarins, according to the theme, stepping out of the cars and marching up our pathway clutching bottles in one hand and all manner of musical instruments in the other—from guitars to African tom-toms—if we had not had the forethought to invite them, too. If they did not accept, at least they had been warned, for the festivities went on until the small hours of the morning and summer parties took the form of barbecues preceded by a garden fete, often attended by about seventy guests. At the barbecues held in the copse at the end of the garden the men did the cooking; in fact they did the whole thing, for they also arranged fairy lights in the trees, Chinese lanterns, and laid on a cable to play the tape recorder on which, as one of my small contributions I had prerecorded suitable background music.

Not being a party person myself I nevertheless did my bit in the name

43

of charity and loyalty to one's flesh and blood. I usually made two other contributions. One was to hold competitions; these took the form of puzzles stuck around the walls with fiendishly difficult clues which I took great delight in compiling. They were extremely unpopular as no one could ever solve them. Nevertheless they added many sixpences to the funds and kept down the cost of prizes which rarely had to be handed out. I, also, with the help of a crony with similar tastes dispensed drinks from a bar set up in the hall. This effort was much more popular—especially with the two of us. Guests on arrival were offered a choice of punch or fruit cup. In the room behind the bar we mixed our concoctions, and, as Gibby considered himself a connoisseur, we naturally had to do much tasting to make sure that we did not offend the palates of our clientele. Around 11 p.m. without fail my party spirit evaporated rapidly. So much so, although there were some who gave a different explanation, that it became imperative for me to have a cat-nap. Like Churchill, I told myself. I also convinced myself that as parties were going on in different rooms—cards in one, music in another, parlour games in a third and chit-chat in the kitchen, hall and other odd corners—I would not be missed if I detached myself from the festivities and had a quiet nap. Unfortunately certain astute friends nosed their way to my room almost as though a trail had been laid. Although my bedroom was quite small it housed an impressive amount of possessions. One wall was lined by a huge bookcase which our elder brother, many years ago, had cleverly constructed from an old-fashioned kitchen dresser. It was crowned by rows of gallon jars of fermenting home-made wine. The room also served as a dark-room and in addition to an enlarger, a kitchen cabinet full of photographic equipment and chemicals graced the wall at the foot of my divan for which there was only just room. On this divan, a fugitive from the party, I reclined like a latter day Cleopatra holding court with friends who wanted to discuss photography, winemaking or, the more scholastic ones, books. After about an hour's relaxation in the prone position I was ready to re-join the fray until it broke up, usually about 3 a.m. Babs on the other hand was quite indefatigable; she glided from room to room, handing round her delicious concoctions, looking radiant to the end, and still having enough vitality left when all was over to calculate how much her pet charity had benefited.

Who would run the parties indeed? Last year Cyril and Doreen came to see us on the island. After affectionate kisses all round Doreen said "Do you know we haven't had a single party since you left!"

A few days after our return home school re-opened and, to give the full term's notice necessary, Babs tendered her resignation to Surrey County Council. For the first time this, more than anything else so far, brought home to us the enormity of our undertaking. In addition to having to find the money, for negotiations to buy the island were going well ahead, we had now cut off our main source of income. Whoever heard of a pensioner underwriting the costs of buying an island? and the shares I intended to sell were hardly likely to rock the Stock Exchange.

The outlook did look a trifle bleak. Mr Nancollas had asked if he could try to sell our house for us. It did not seem a good idea as he was so far away, but we nevertheless agreed to let him have a go. Weeks went by during which we did not have a single enquiry about the house and although Babs had written to both Cornwall and Devon Education Authorities and scoured the *Times Educational Supplement* every week there was apparently not a single teacher's vacancy in the West country. We were not actually downcast. The idea of living on an island was so thrilling that we were still inclined to push these major problems into the background and concentrate on the, to us, more important aspects, such as what equipment we would need to take with us. Babs for instance made a sortie up to Chelsea and acquired a magnificent stone-cutting and polishing machine from a firm who supplied the experts; archaeologists, university expeditions and the like. It cost just over £120. It would pay dividends, she said. In any case, we both agreed, it was a good capital investment. It must be admitted, however, that "capital investment" was a term we always trotted out to justify the purchase of anything which seemed essential to us at the time.

I already owned a Mamiyaflex camera with three supplementary lenses, ideal for the kind of general freelance work I had been doing. But the telephoto lens had not sufficient focal length for the bird photography which would be an obvious "must" in our future life. A Pentax camera that would take a 400-mm lens seemed to be the answer. This supplementary lens is about one foot long and had the added bonus that it could also be used as a portable telescope. Then an Olympus "Pen" EE, a miniature camera that could be slipped into one's pocket, and would take 72 half frames would be ideal for "note-taking". Eventually one would knock up oil paintings from it for which the whole art world would be clamouring—of course! Acquiring this "essential" equipment knocked me back about £150, but in fact, according to my reckoning, cost me nothing, for I had made an unwritten law that any money I earned from photography would be ploughed back into photographic equipment. This way I had something to show for all the hours spent in the darkroom until 4 a.m. and paying extra income tax for the privilege of doing so. To help fill in the time profitably I also enrolled at the Art School for Photography.

But silence continued on the housing and scholastic side, broken only by the Wailing Winnies chorus of our friends. We, too, sometimes had our moments of doubt and despair. It is difficult to ride the crest of a wave all the time.

It was during one of these sloughs of despondency, on a Friday lunch-time, that Babs rang me from school, her voice choked with emotion. My heart thudded. She never telephoned from school so it must be serious. Instantly I knew—she couldn't stand the worry and suspense any longer. "God! she's going to jump in the river" was the thought that leapt through my mind, although there wasn't a river for miles around.

"What is it?" I quavered, my throat tight with fear.

"There's an advertisement in the Times Educational Supplement," she stuttered, "for a senior mistress . . . Guess where? . . . LOOE!" She couldn't believe her eyes nor I my ears. Surely this was Fate!

In a daze she sent off for the application forms, returned them complete with references and testimonials, and awaited the outcome in a state of animated suspension. The mechanics of life went on but we might as well have been puppets on a string for all the world about us cared.

Then one day a letter plopped on to the door mat; she had been short-listed for an interview. Although this was a terrific piece of good luck the tension did not lessen; if anything it increased. The waiting time until the fateful day stretched agonisingly on. "Maybe it's a foregone conclusion job," said Babs ominously, "and I am called to make up the numbers." We went off our food again, although it did not make any difference to our weights—it never did.

At last the day for the interview drew near. We travelled down to Cornwall after school, making this unscheduled trip in a fever of excitement and fear. We swore that Toby could have driven the car, since he had made the journey so many times. He had an uncanny way of knowing when we crossed the border from Devon to Cornwall whether at Gunnislake or over the river Tamar, whether by daylight or in darkness. As soon as we approached the border he would be up on his hind legs, paws up on the front seat, waving his gorgeous tail and barking joyously. He never evinced such excitement crossing the border in the reverse direction; nevertheless he acknowledged the transition by taking up his usual stance, leaning forward with his paws on the front seat but merely peering through the window and giving a faint swish of his curly tail to signify that we were over the border. Every owner, of course, has the cleverest dog in the whole wide world. We were no exception. This time, however, we registered only a glimmer of pride as the usual shouts of delight took us over the Tamar in the darkness and into Cornwall. If people had seen our strained faces they would have thought that we were on the run from a big London bank robbery at least.

We slept restlessly in the cottage that night. Whereas the rosy glow of our early dreams of living on an island had clouded our minds to facing harsh facts, the importance of the outcome of the interview had brought them sharply into focus. The interview was in the afternoon but, as is usual, the chosen applicants are allowed to look over the school beforehand and ask any questions they wish. Babs brought me breakfast in bed preparatory to driving up to the school, about a mile out of Looe. I couldn't eat it. I was ill, feverish with headache and bad tummy pains. We tried to share the food but Babs couldn't eat anything either so we gave up. Bab was gone most of the morning while I stayed in bed dozing fitfully. At last I heard her footsteps, her high heels dragging over the cobblestones in the courtyard. "No hope, then," I muttered to myself into the pillow. She came into the bedroom and immediately burst into tears. I joined in. Between sobs she told me that she didn't stand a chance. The post was for the senior mistress, but the subject that went with it was needlework and one of the other candidates was the needlework expert for the whole of Hampshire or some such county; another candidate was the resident domestic science mistress. Although Babs was qualified in needlework, having taken it at college, the post she had just vacated did not include teaching officially, even if filling in due to illness gave her a wide variety of experience. The technical claims on the needlework score of these two candidates were greater than her own and this she felt would carry the day.

Babs repaired her face, smartened herself up again and bravely set off once more for the afternoon's ordeal, while I buried myself in the bedclothes again, trying to quell the nausea and sickness that prevented even dozing this time. Wild thoughts raced through my feverish brain. Would this astounding opportunity be dangled before her eyes only to be snatched away at the last? I couldn't bear the agony of waiting and eventually fell into a nightmarish half sleep. Suddenly the bang of the car door being slammed awakened me. I heard Babs's footsteps tapping quickly and lightly over the cobbles and I knew she had the job. She burst into the room and we hugged each other as she told me that she had been appointed, that it must have been her senior position and experience that had filled the bill and she was to take up the appointment next term after the Christmas holiday. An extraordinary coincidence was that the vacancy had been caused by the resignation of a member of staff who, after years of teaching at the school, had suddenly announced her forthcoming marriage. The engagement must have taken place just about the time when we first had the opportunity of buying the island. Jubilant beyond measure we celebrated by having a slap-up meal, the first for weeks, for, as soon as I knew that the job was hers, my symptoms disappeared miraculously and I jumped out of bed completely cured. Moneywise Babs would drop several hundreds of pounds a year by giving up her deputy headship for, although this was the senior mistress's post, the school was less than a third the size of the one she had left, but, as we had said many times, who would not do this if it meant having a stake in paradise, for so our island seemed to us? It was an incredible stroke of good fortune that Babs should have landed this job for it was an excellent one indeed and surely fate must have taken a hand in arranging that it was only a ship's hawser length from the island, in a manner of speaking. We recrossed the Tamar once more and as Toby swished his tail and peered through the window at Devon we both shouted "Good Boy! CLEVER BOY! Toby."

Back in Surrey we decided that we must do something about selling the house ourselves as so far we had not had a single enquiry and it was now October. Accordingly we dropped a note to Mr Nancollas and put the house in the hands of several local agents. It was not at that time a sellers' market and we did not get a single bite, but this did not worry us unduly, for we were great believers in property as an investment and hoped that in the course of time ours would get the fairly high price we were asking. It was a good detached property near the famous Epsom Downs racecourse and had a lovely garden, part of it landscaped by a friend, Graham Jones, with standard roses leading to an archway of ramblers; this led through from the lawn and flower borders to fruit trees, more lawn, vegetable patch and so to a copse where it was a delight to swing in a hammock, with the sun dappling one's face, listening to bird song and the murmur of insects and the breeze rippling through the leaves. We had moved here some ten years before after mother developed heart trouble and the doctor said that we should move her away from the large rambling house in which we then lived, with its many stairs and steps, to somewhere more compact and on the level. While she was still alive we had added every modern convenience we could think of, including night storage heaters, which at that time were an innovation. We had a "treasure", Mrs Penman, who came three hours every day, and a gardener of the old school who tended the garden one day a week. Although there was the beautiful Surrey countryside on our doorstep and it was possible to drive to the coast without passing through a single town there was actually a bus stop outside the front gate to take one to Banstead village or on to Sutton. No wonder our friends thought that we were mad to give up all this to live alone on an island off the wild coast of Cornwall, especially as we were not exactly youthful specimens of the weaker sex.

In other directions events began to move rather rapidly. Completion date for the purchase of the island drew near. This would mean yet another trip to Cornwall to sign the documents—whether a personal visit was strictly necessary I cannot remember—but we arranged that we should in fact travel down there to do so during Babs' October half-term holiday. It seemed incredible that it was just one year ago that we had, on the spur of the moment, during this self-same holiday gone down to Cornwall to look for a cottage. Now we not only had two cottages but were about to acquire an island as well. We had asked Mr Browning, the solicitor, to make the actual date for signing 21st October, this being Trafalgar Day. There were certain naval traditions in the family that made this date seem appropriate and desirable. Our father had served in the Merchant Navy, our younger brother had volunteered for and served in the Royal Navy and, during the war, I had been fortunate to serve in the W.R.N.S.

Meantime we had to find the rest of the money. There was still no sign of selling the house at our figure. Most of the agents wanted us to drop our price considerably in order to make a quick sale. This we refused to do. We needed our asking price and we felt sure that, if we waited, the pendulum would swing and it would become a seller's market. It was also a poor time for selling shares. My stockbroker, whose imagination was caught by this wildly romantic idea of buying an island, said that he would get the best price he could when the right moment came and he would sell only those shares that would make a profit. Babs luckily had a nest egg and this together with a bridging loan advanced by our friendly bank manager at the Westminster took care of the immediate financial problems.

"You will sell the cottages of course?" said a male acquaintance, rather pompously, not caring much for the idea of women venturing into the realms of high finance and property deals with any prospect of success.

"We had not envisaged doing so," we replied just as pompously. In fact we still had it in mind that, just as in "Monopoly", we would turn over the cards and mortgage them if absolutely necessary. But to sell, No! For one thing Babs would need one cottage as a *pied á terre*. The other cottage, which would no longer be needed as a pottery, we decided we would furnish completely, and let for summer holidays. This would provide the extra income we felt sure we would need for the maintenance of the island, for we did not see ourselves as full-time market gardeners, if at all. For another thing we were natural hoarders. We loved buying and acquiring things, but we were loathe to part with our possessions once they were ours. "Might come in useful one day," the litany of all hoarders, was ours also. It certainly applied to the cottages. Apart from anything else, we had a great affection for them and for the life we had made among the folk around, many of whom had become our friends.

So in high spirits we made this, our penultimate journey from Surrey to Cornwall, for completion date formalities. Mr Whitehouse had asked if we would be willing to make a covenant with the National Trust to protect the island from commercial development during any future ownership. To this we readily and eagerly agreed for we too were anxious that this beautiful unspoilt gem should never be exploited for commercial gain. Mr Browning did point out that, otherwise, future owners might not experience too much difficulty in obtaining planning permission for certain developments, as the geographical position of the island, its size, lack of mainland services or public transport made economic self sufficiency virtually impossible. We had heard that at earlier changes of ownership Looe Council had turned down opportunities to purchase, even when the price was fairly minimal, no doubt realising that its upkeep would be a drain on the rates. Previous owners apparently all had private means or, apart from the revenue from market gardening, some other form of income, as in our modest way we also would have.

So come Trafalgar Day, 1964, unbelievably the island would be ours.

The Whitehouses had moved to the mainland back in the summer, so the weather being fair and the sea calm we hired a boatman to take us across. First we sailed right round our future home taking photographs.

Although only 22½ acres the island, with its indented coastline, appeared much larger. The west coast, wild and rugged and remote looked like a Land's End in miniature. Here, above the forbidding cliffs of rock and caves, the island rose to a height of 150 feet. On the north and east the wooded hillside sloped steeply down to cliffs above shelving beaches of rock, sand and shingle. The south coast, like the west, was buttressed with perpendicular rocky cliffs but sloped down to a promontory on the south-eastern tip where it was joined to the little island by a stone bridge. It was here that the tabernacle for the flagstaff that we had mistaken for a rival purchaser stood, a lonely sentinel against the skyline. The trees that bordered the cliffs of the eastern shore and climbed the slopes of the hill that crowned the island were a blaze of reds, oranges and gold as the leaves gleamed in the autumn sunlight.

We landed for a short time and were amazed to find outdoor tomatoes ripening, the trusses heavy with fruit; butterflies fluttered among huge clusters of blackberries along the hedgerows and, incredibly, we had to take off our jackets and walk in short-sleeved summer dresses as we walked down the cliff path to the little island. And this was late afternoon near the end of October. We had stepped into another world. We were in time to see a most spectacular sunset from the bridge. The lichen-covered rocks below us and the dramatic cliffs of the southern coastline glowed gold, purple and wondrous shades of rose in the rays of the setting sun far out in the Atlantic. The swooping seagulls screamed above the murmur of the sea and the only sign of human life was our future home, a white house on the cliff top above us. We were relieved to note that although the house stood only a few yards from the cliff edge to the south and another cliff on the other side, the hill rose steeply behind it; this not only protected it from the west but gave the house an air of solid security, no doubt due to the psychological confidence inspired by being positioned with its "back to the wall" .

Back on the mainland we had a few ends to tie up with Mr Nancollas who had undertaken to make an inventory of the lock, stock and barrel. Included were farming machinery, a caterpillar tractor being the most important, and among many other items of equipment three boats and some outboard engines. It hadn't escaped our notice that two of our three wishes had now come true in a most miraculous way.

"Milk store, here we come!" we said over a celebratory drink, as though it mattered now. Nevertheless that wish too was granted although we had no inkling at that time that one day it would be.

As Babs had a bit of holiday in hand we stayed on a day or two and set about buying some suitable clothing for our future life. First we equipped ourselves with weatherproof anoraks, oilskins and sou'westers; we then visited Mr Toms of East Looe to be fitted out with sea boots. There was a twofold reason for visiting him, for in addition to selling the kind of foot-gear we wanted, he also had a son, Wren Toms, whom we understood usually did the ferrying of furniture and equipment for the island and this was the only way we knew of contacting him.

"Yes! you will certainly need Wren," said Mr Toms. "I will tell him."

Hindsight would have told us that it was probable that the whole of East and West Looe, including Wren Toms, knew our intentions and re-quirements but, ignorant of this, we were only too happy to know that this important person would be made aware that we should like the use of his skilled services at Christmastide, even though the request was by proxy.

Rather pleased with our purchases which were in striking contrast to the fashionable wearing apparel we were in the habit of buying for our business efficiency and modern smart teacher acts respectively, we, for the last time, we hoped, returned to Surrey.

There everything worked up to a crescendo of excitement and activity. Dennis and An O'Neill had arranged that I could attend Art School all day and every day whenever possible so that I could have the maximum of tuition and practice. One day I was throwing on the wheel from 9 a.m. until 9 p.m. In a coma of exhaustion I tottered off to catch the bus as Babs was not available to collect me, to find later that the O'Neills were search-ing for me everywhere to run me home as they thought that I looked like passing out on the wheel, and feared that in fact I had done so in some dark corner. Heaven knows how Babs coped with the Christmas term with the move dominating our lives. There were the school and form Christmas parties, carol singing, Christmas Fayre, parents' evening and, as was usual at her school, an ambitious and highly successful Gilbert and Sullivan production. Babs I think was responsible for the costumes or make-up or both and she was in a frenzy of school activity the whole term.

Moving at any time for any family is a nightmare. We had our special problems that sent us demented. What should we take that could go over the sea in an open boat in winter time, and, being compulsive hoarders, what should we sell that would not cause us future heartbreak? Mr Nancollas had offered us the use of his store on the quayside under his office but that would be only a temporary haven as he needed it for his fortnightly auction sales. Luckily most of our big furniture had been sold on our previous move from the old house but we still had some heavy stuff. We had some dealers who instantly made a bee-line for the antiques, and if we agreed to sell them they would take anything else more or less as a favour—at knock down prices, of course. So we tried out a few pieces at auction sales but the prices offered came nowhere near their value. This exercise was a mistake anyway, as we found ourselves buying things instead, which only added to our problem. In the end we decided to keep the antiques to furnish No 1 cottage, taking the more manageable ones over to the island. The big furniture we would sell privately by advertising. To our surprise we had sold everything we advertised in next to no time. Everything went at the asking price with no quibbling at all. We supposed that would-be purchasers would not come unless they wanted to buy and, furthermore, they could see where the articles came from, unlike the anonymous pedigree of those offered in sales. Whatever the reason it solved that problem.

There were other problems in plenty. I had 40 gallons of wine fermenting and these we decided were a "must" to go sailing over the sea—likewise the many hundreds of books we possessed and were considered essential. Babs and I had so far agreed over every major issue, often without the need to consult each other, buying cottages and an island for starters. But as is often the case in families we disagreed over something quite trivial. Not that it was trivial physically. The bone of contention was the enormous bookcase in my bedroom. We did not actually argue about it—it was just that at regular intervals Babs said flatly that it was too big to go and I just as doggedly said that I was not leaving it behind. In the end we reached a compromise—we would leave it to the carriers to decide. So when the manager came to give an estimate for the removal later he said that everything would just go into two pantechnicons and the bookcase could go if there were room at the last.

"If so," said Babs philosophically, "it can always be sold at one of Mr Nancollas's auction sales—it will be in the right place."

Meantime with more buying time available than Babs, I acquired other items that I thought might come in useful in our future life. Among these was an electric drill with all the attachments, including a lathe and an electric saw, all of which frightened me to death as I had never been the slightest bit mechanical. Marjorie's brother came over and demonstrated them to me and like a conjurer made the whole operation seem like child's play (Marjorie was the friend who had been staying with us in the cottage when I first set eyes on the island on that momentous early morning walk at Whitsun). I also made a trip to London and bought an Adana printing machine, after a demonstration by a young man who did it with a flair that again made me feel that I was watching a conjuring trick to which I could never aspire. Maybe he thought so too. However, I had seen really excellent results from the efforts of children at Babs' school exhibition so I thought that perhaps its manipulation would not be quite beyond me. I also bought a hurricane lamp from Blacks, the tent people. Here I plucked up courage to ask about getting a discount as I had just read an article in a newspaper which advised one to do this when buying equipment. Why I chose the purchase of a hurricane lamp as a guinea pig it is hard to fathom as of all our purchases it was a comparatively minor item, but to my surprise it worked, in a way. The assistant asked, "Just *one* hurricane lamp?" "Well," I added hurriedly, "later I shall probably want another, or even two more." "Then I suggest you get those from our warehouse where they deal wholesale. Here is an invoice for this one. Send it with your next order to this address, where they will allow you a discount on this one too." And with this the helpful assistant wrote down the address and handed me the slip.

Emboldened by this success I put the same question at my next port of call, an electronics shop in the Edgware Road. Their impressive display of tape recorders in the window had attracted my attention many times on my way to my dentist in a Square just off Marble Arch. I already owned a fine stereo tape recorder that, if you shut your eyes when listening to it, gave the illusion that you were actually at a concert in the Festival Hall. That, in fact, would have been a better place to house it for it was so large and heavy, being a prototype and manufactured just before transistors streamlined such equipment, that it always needed a strong man to move it. What I now wanted to complement it was a small portable one for recording bird song. Transistor models of these the shop had in plenty and when I enquired about them someone was called forth from behind the scenes to deal with me. He must have thought that I intended buying the lot for no other claimants to his time got a look in. As to discount, he pointed out that as retailers they could not deal wholesale but he could let me have 5%. I was so pleased about this that I told him where I intended using it. This had repercussions for this was not the last time I was to hear from this gentleman who, it transpired, was a visiting director. The tale of how Eric Cox came to stay on the island must be told later.

I wished I had read the article about asking for discounts earlier for I had already ordered a cement mixing machine, a greenhouse heater, a soil sterilizing stove and a brick-making machine. Although we had disposed of two three-piece suites, two bedroom suites, a hall stand and other fairly large items of furniture, the place was beginning to look like a warehouse as almost daily fresh parcels and packing cases of new equipment arrived.

"We shall need three pantechnicons soon!" cried Babs in desperation. Her stone cutting and polishing machine was a really large affair with a built-in stand so this she had arranged to have delivered to the store in Looe. I did likewise with the potters' wheel I had ordered through John Shelly. This was a large traditional kick-wheel made by a Dorset wheel-wright to John Shelly's own design and was similar to the one I had used on his course.

"Anyway the telescope won't take up much room," I consoled Babs. We were delighted with this. One starry night we tried it out. We were amazed to find that the very first star we pointed at was not a star at all but the planet Saturn with the rings plainly visible. It was a thrilling sight and sent us buying even more books on astronomy to add to those we already had.

We also bought a Kenwood Chef mixer with many attachments from the area rep., a charming fellow who afterwards invited us to his place at Guildford for drinks and coffee and, indeed, he too has been to visit us on the island, not to sell anything for there were no more attachments left to buy. We bought, too, a "Sunbeam" cooking pan and a mass of other kitchenware we thought would be useful in a farmhouse kitchen. In addition, we already had most of the gadgets and equipment that annually tempted us at the Ideal Home Exhibition. One would think that we were about to colonize an uninhabited country with no hope of ever seeing the motherland again. In the event nearly all these acquisitions proved invaluable and saved us much time and money. The two exceptions were the greenhouse heater which became redundant for the simple reason that due to the mild climate of the island the greenhouse, even in the depth of winter, never needed heating. The other was the cement mixer. It was not that it was incapable of doing the job. On the contrary, it was most efficient. Nor was cement mixing as a way of life in our calculations wrongly forecast. Year in and year out cement is mixed up even more often than farmhouse puddings. But I had overlooked two important points, for it must be admitted that buying the cement mixer was my abortive brain child. The first was that I would not have time to do everything. Although I loved using that mixer it did take me away from pottery and other crafts. Secondly, I could not persuade anyone else to use it. It would appear that any first class worker suspects anything that smacks of gadgetry, and especially mistrustful are country folk. All our helpers prefer to keep to the spit and shovel method, finding it perhaps more satisfying. Not so Paul Shelley, the greengrocer in the middle of Market Square in West Looe. He asked if he could buy it from me. Although I found it useful for mixing up compost I was very happy that it would be put to its rightful use and recently swopped it with him for a custom-built bookcase in parana pine, and very elegant it looks.

The manager from the carriers had said that we need not pack a thing apart from our personal belongings. His men would bring packing cases and do the lot. So the problem now was that if ever we really moved from Surrey we should need a packer just for our private belongings, for neither of us has ever been able to travel light or live neatly. Most of our friends are the type who, if they come for the day carry, apart from the regulation bunch of flowers, nothing else at all. A weekend visitor brings nothing more than an airline type handgrip inside which there is still enough room for a hostess gift of whisky or gin. If we visit their homes unexpectedly you would think that a glossy magazine staff was awaited any moment to do a feature article, or that the Queen might drop in. If ever anyone knocks on *our* door unexpectedly, redfaced we cower in a corner among a heterogeneous collection of possessions, and hiss at each other, "We're OUT! WE'RE OUT!" We cannot even go to bed without taking enough impedimenta for a fortnight's holiday and making several journeys into the bargain. My particular choice of essentials usually comprises three books, four magazines, a tape recorder, pocket radio, notebook and pencil, throat pastilles, hot drink, hand cream and nail file. By the time that little lot are organised, all of which are supposed to be conducive to sleep, one is out like a light before one's head has so much as touched the pillow. Small wonder then that we queried how we should ever move from Surrey. Luckily Doug, our niece's husband, who had spent Boxing Day with us in the cottage had offered to come up from Saltdean, where they lived, to do our private packing for us. And Doug had been in the Navy. It reminded me of the time when I was in the W.R.N.S. and had to leave Scotland, where I had spent my service so far, to go to O.T.C. at Greenwich Naval College.

I had accumulated so many belongings that I thought it would be better if I had stayed in Scotland for the duration.

"Leave everything to me," said the Chief Petty Officer who was throwing a farewell party for me. "Don't pack a thing apart from your suitcase." The next day seven naval ratings appeared with a Leading Hand in charge. In no time at all seventeen boxes all roped up in true naval fashion were stowed on to the waiting R.N. transport, the top crowned with a bicycle and portable stove. Naval parties being what they are it was as well that, as I giddily headed south the next day, I only had the responsibility of a suitcase. When I was finally due to leave the W.R.N.S. accommodation stowage space had grown with promotion, and the question of removal had grown so acute that I was greatly tempted to accept the invitation of their Lordships of the Admiralty to sign on for life so that I should not have to face the problem. However, the Navy came to the rescue again, headed by "Chippy", who made me an enormous ditty box that is with me to this day, and aided by the Supply Officer, First Lieutenant and many others who possibly thought that the Royal Navy could sail the Seven Seas without my help, I just about made Civvy Street.

It was a great relief therefore when Doug said he would do our packing for us. Our faith was justified. History repeated itself and after a few weekends the most precious of our multifarious possessions and the fruits of our many activities were neatly stowed in boxes, expertly roped and meticulously labelled. The way was now clear for the carriers to deal with the more usual Lares and Penates.

This was not the end of our worries however. One that we had not bargained for was the problem of the island cat. The Whitehouses had written previously to ask if we could take up residence earlier as the gardener's cat had refused to leave the island. Their daughter had been rowing over once a week to leave it food. Now they wrote again as the autumn gales had started and no one could get out to feed her. We, of course, could do nothing about it for Babs was committed until the end of term. We were 240 miles away and the move, which could only be compared with the evacuation of Dunkirk with the outcome just as certain, still lay ahead. Nevertheless we were sick with worry thinking about the cat as we listened to weather reports and heard that heavy seas were pounding the south west coasts continuously.

We supposed, too, that we should have worried that at this late stage we not only had not sold the house but no one had even come to view it.

The agents continued to pester us to drop the price but as we had had it valued we waited hopefully for the swing of the pendulum to make it a seller's market again. As we had a bridging loan we pushed this particular problem to the back of our minds. At least it gave Cyril plenty of time to do some more decorating so that it would be in tip-top order when we left. Not that the house really needed it. I doubt if any property had been painted more often than ours. We were always changing the colour scheme and helpful friends lightened the burden. I, personally, found painting therapeutic. When I had problems, and they were always looming up like leering fish, painting provided a nice cow-like occupation and the care, attention to detail and the rhythmic movements required, put any current problems in nice perspective.

Babs had many talented and helpful friends and faithfully they now rallied round. Mac was an educational officer in a remand home and a major in the Territorials and his particular skill was electricity. He always installed our gadgets for us and if anything ever went wrong he would be round like a shot and, pipe in mouth, would get whatever it was working again in a very careful and deliberate way. He undertook to remove chandeliers, wall brackets and other fitments we wished to take with us and leave everything in good order for the next inhabitants. Johnny was another faithful standby. A headmaster, secretary of the county N.U.T., and a former test pilot he could nevertheless always be relied on to come round and deal with anything electronic, plumbing problems and anything to do with engines and machinery. Jane, his wife, who came round to collect him one evening sometime before this, said with hardly any trace of bitterness, "I suppose you know that while Johnny has been round here mending your leaking taps I have had to decorate the back bedroom and replumb our bathroom myself!"

Now everyone started to throw farewell parties for us. The cry, in addition to "What are you going to do without your friends?" (which had become a theme song), alternated with, "What are you going to do without a man?", which was more to the point. Well, we hoped that the Lord would provide, preferably in the plural, when the need arose. In our youth, although it had been spent at different times, we were lucky enough to have two older brothers who were always on hand to do anything required. In adult life we were naive enough to expect that others would be only too willing to take on this role—a habit we had never quite shaken off. Consequently we had no fears for the future and brushed our friends' forebodings aside with lighthearted insouciance. In any case we had discovered that most men at heart are knights in shining armour who will tilt a lance on one's behalf if they are allowed, even if the dragon is only a leaking tap.

Not that we were lacking in offers. Doug was ready to chuck up everything and join us with his family. Mr Nancollas had written to say that he had several applicants who would like to work on the island for us and asked if he should arrange interviews for when we came down. The word had certainly got around, for we began to receive letters ourselves from a variety of people offering their services. One reason for this was the fact that quite unexpectedly a local Surrey paper came out with the banner headline "SURREY TEACHER BUYS ISLAND!" and there was a photograph of Babs and a long front page feature. We couldn't understand the furore that followed and thought that the sooner we moved the better. We had enough on our plate worrying about the possibly starving cat without being responsible for humans who would certainly starve if we took on the flocks that wanted to join us. One man and his wife persuaded us to let them come and see us. They seemed an ideal couple and we almost came to an arrangement with them but luckily the idea fell through. We had promised Doug that we would give him a chance later if we found that there could be any future for him. As he was a young chap with many skills who could turn his hand to anything he certainly would be a great asset to us. Meantime we felt we must fashion our own future.

Moving day drew near and the sorting out of possessions became more frantic. Jumble sales and the Christmas Fair at the nearby church did very well out of us for in the end we were tossing out valuable wares in our frenzy. Violet Jordan, a friend I had made at the Art School, came to say goodbye and left bedazzled with a dozen evening dresses and ball gowns of Babs, which we assured her would not be needed on the island. The logic of why she therefore needed them eluded Violet, especially as none of them fitted her, but at least it got one little burden off our hands. The gift of a huge five gallon glass carboy to Graham was much better received. He intended to grow an indoor garden in it and if he were as successful with this as he had been with our rose garden he would soon have a flourishing display.

Among the farewell gifts we received none was more treasured than a book on vegetable growing presented to me by Ernie, the gardener. It was very old and must have been in his family since the turn of the century.

Nevertheless it was the most comprehensive book on vegetables I have ever seen. Each variety, and there were some quite unknown to me, had a chapter to itself. The information given included planting times, distances to sow, seed germination time, life of seeds, estimated crops per ounce and per pound of seed, yield per yard and acre, sowing and planting calendar, the effects of different soils, climates, pests and diseases and how to deal with them and hints on harvesting, storing and cooking. In addition to all this each chapter started off with a potted history including the earliest known references to that particular vegetable. Quotations were given from the Bible, Pliny, Herodotus, the Elizabethan poets and others, and included such fascinating details as the fact that Herodotus had seen a reference to a sale of onions inscribed on the Great Pyramid. As he presented me with the book from his gnarled hands Ernie's face creased with pride. He also gave me a parting piece of advice, "Allus go in for early crops and anything yer can grow out of season. That way it's highest returns for least labour." He should know, for one of their specialities used to be growing strawberries exclusively for Wimbledon and Ascot week.

Farewells were made to winemaking pupils, National Savings groups clientele and colleagues, neighbours, all at the Art School, the doctor, hairdresser, local shopkeepers and the small boy who haunted the house, and helped in the darkroom, who said longingly how he was going to miss the "house of gadgets". Farewell, too, to my friends at Hall's and Babs to all her friends and colleagues from the many facets of her professional life. Most spoke as though we were leaving for outer space and were going into orbit forever. I did consider calling in at the Labour Exchange to say goodbye but in view of the proclivity I had for confusing everyone there it seemed prudent to give that particular call a miss. I might have found myself with another job and unable to leave Surrey after all.

Most of the parties were over and there only remained the grand farewell dinner our friends were giving for us. We had even disposed, one way and another, of all our goods "surplus to requirements". Among these was an electric mower which Phil Odd, the brother-in-law of my school friend Tommy, was going to buy from us. He came up to collect it the day before we were due to move. We happened to mention to him that we had received a letter that morning from the firm of Miles, an agent for flowers in Covent Garden. Mr Miles had written to say that he understood that we were taking over from Mr Whitehouse and that he hoped we would continue to deal with his firm. This had given us cold feet. Our knowledge of daffodils was restricted to the few dozen that we grew in the garden and we thought that all daffodils were the same—*yellow*. We were nonplussed when we knew that fifteen different varieties were grown on the island and that they bloomed in succession from Christmas until early April. We found the prospect of marketing them daunting especially as we understood that Milés was one of the largest agents in Covent Garden. We were confiding all this to Phil when to our immense surprise he said he knew the family well and had been friendly with the daughter since schooldays. He phoned Covent Garden straight away. Mr Miles had left the office so Phil got through to his home and introduced us over the telephone. Mr Miles was very charming indeed. He told us not to worry at all and that he would give us any help and advice we needed. This cheered us up enormously and we now felt that we had at least one anchorage in the sea of uncertainty of our future life.

Although the preparations for our removal had assumed a nightmarish quality moving day itself went incredibly smoothly. Thirty packing cases of books, forty gallon jars of wine, one full five-gallon carboy, innumerable crates and the roped and labelled boxes as well as the furniture were swallowed by the giant pantechnicon as though a ravenous monster was being expertly fed by a team of men who were specially trained to exude calm and confidence in an electrically charged atmosphere. Carriers must be a resilient race when you consider that their whole working life, when not spent in pounding along the main roads, is occupied in meeting people who are in various stages of overwrought nerves bordering on hysteria.

Garden equipment was to follow later and was stowed in the garden shed and garage. As well as the usual impedimenta of tools there were three mowers, a roller, hammock, garden seats, deck chairs, bird tables, lawn pricker, fertiliser dispenser and a recently acquired cedar wood shed. Mrs Penman, the treasure, was left in charge. She was going to give the house a thorough clean, get rid of rubbish and, most important of all, was appointed to deal with estate agents. Sadly, if there was not room for the bookcase, she was to sell it for us.

Anxiously I watched as the cavernous belly of the pantechnicon began to fill up until it seemed there was hardly room to shut the doors. At last the bookcase was the only piece left. With a cheery wink at me the foreman said "Just about room for that I think." And the gigantic beast outside gobbled down this huge tid-bit, clamped its jaws and rumbled off. It was to take two days for the journey and as the day was fairly advanced we too decided to make the trip in two stages. With final waves to friends, neighbours and Mrs Penman we set off on the first stage of our big adventure.

Chapter 4

Entr'acte—a link with the past

As we sped westward and our former life receded into the past with every mile we travelled we marvelled at the twists and turns of fate that had brought us on this exciting adventure. Most of our friends could not understand why we should want to uproot ourselves from our comfortable home and from all our friends for the uncertainties, privations and loneliness of life on an island, especially when the days of our youth, when roughing it might have had a certain allure, were left far behind. If there was one simple answer it could be said to be parentage, and farther back even than that.

In the latter part of the last century and the days of sail, William, our father, at the age of thirteen ran away to sea, aided and abetted by his grandmother, who, of the opinion that her grandson was being spoilt and brought up too soft by his mother, gave him a gold sovereign and a gold watch to speed him on his way.

He sailed to the Americas, rounded Cape Horn high up in the rigging, one moment borne dizzily aloft and the next almost touching the tremendous seas. Nothing would induce him to go home again, although his father tried to entice him back with the offer of another gold watch and other gifts. Eventually his father promised that if he would come back he would have him trained for the sea. At this the young William returned home and was duly enrolled and joined the training ship *Arethusa* in the Thames and later completed his training at Greenwich Naval College. Among the family papers is a letter written to him on board the *Arethusa* by Lord Jersey wishing him and "my other young friends on the *Arethusa* success in your careers" and inviting them to visit him and Lady Jersey in Australia. Among the papers there is also a certificate stating that Petty Officer William John Edwin Atkins—1 Good Conduct Badge—"could reef, able to furl small sails, heave the lead and give soundings, make bends, knots and splices, could pull in a boat . . ." Written in the Commanding Officer's own hand was the added comment "Conduct Very Good Indeed." Petty Officer

William John Edwin was just sixteen years old.

At sea again he landed in America and wishing to explore that country, he hoboed across the continent travelling from coast to coast slung under the couplings of trains and stopping off as the fancy took him. For a time he became a cowboy. The rich owner of the ranch offered him a good berth if he would stay but William still yearned for the sea and set sail once more.

He also yearned for his childhood sweetheart. From the days when as schoolchildren they had attended services at the lovely old church in Carshalton village in Surrey he had lost his heart to Alice and his dearest hope was that one day she would marry him. Unfortunately for him most other young males felt the same way and had the same aspirations. Young men, top-hatted in the fashion of the day, came to her home to pay court to the lovely young Alice; among them a Frenchman of noble family, and another who, much to the amusement of her sisters, stuck his head through the railings and vowed that he would not go away unless she said that she would be his wife; yet another swore that he would commit suicide if she would not marry him. Although so far, in spite of these impassioned entreaties, none had succeeded in winning her hand, William got to hear about these rivals through his mother who was always trying to come between her son and Alice. Instead of having the desired effect he threatened to leave the sea and come home again; he felt at a disadvantage trying to conduct his courtship from the high seas against what must have seemed to him overwhelming odds.

His grandmother now stepped in again. Among the family papers is an obviously much treasured letter from her to her grandson. In it she implores him not to leave the sea, nor must he listen to these tales, as the young gentleman in question were just friends of the family (which surely must have been the understatement of the century). She felt sorry for Alice who would have a very dull life indeed if she could not go accompanied for walks in the park or be partnered at the skating parties held when the streams and fields were frozen over. She understood Alice, who confided in her. He need not be troubled and therefore he must not do anything foolhardy. Even after all these years it is a very touching letter to read. It was also written in secret. No one must know that she had written to him and his reply must be sent direct to her. We never had the pleasure of meeting this doughty old lady but salute her for the part she played in bringing about our future existence. When one realises that she was alive during the time of the Prince Regent or William IV and would have heard first hand accounts of Nelson and Trafalgar it is not surprising that the sea was in her blood. It also spans the passage of the years and brings those far off distant figures of history vividly close and uncannily alive.

The letter having the desired effect William did not leave the sea and very soon after the longed for answer came at last from Alice. This he received just two weeks before his ship was due to sail for England. Determined that there should be no chance for her to change her mind or for anyone else to do it for her, he immediately applied to the Archbishop of Canterbury for a special licence. The wedding ceremony was to take place at St Anne's, the nearest church to the East India Dock, as soon as his ship berthed there. He appointed his future sister-in-law's husband, George, to be in charge of all arrangements, and then set sail with all speed for England. The wedding party awaiting the arrival of the twenty-one-year-old groom consisted of Alice, her sister and George. Unfortunately the ship was late docking and when they arrived at the church everything was locked up. William and George leapt over the gate and managed to catch the Vicar who, having given them up, had just left. He returned at once, opened up, let them in and performed the Ceremony with only minutes to spare before the prescribed time expired. The captain had arranged the wedding breakfast on board but when Alice saw that she would have to climb up the ship's rope ladder, terrified of heights as she was all her life, she absolutely refused to do so. So instead the wedding party repaired to her home to celebrate, buying a cake on the way.

So William at last won his bride and for the next sixty years, spanning six reigns, in his eyes she was always the girl of twenty he had married in those far off days. Was it the glamour of the sea and his spirit of adventure that gave him the edge over his rivals? We never knew. The most that we could elicit from mother, the most shy and reticent of people, was that in those days he was very good looking and looked very smart in his uniform.

As soon as William was back at sea the rival suitors told Alice that she had made the biggest mistake of her life and one even implored her to elope with him. Alice would listen to none of them; instead she left the parental home of her widowed mother and proceeded to take an apartment in whichever port William was due to dock, this most often being Avonmouth, and there she would sit in the window watching for his ship to come sailing over the horizon.

Apart from the sea, Dad's other great love was cricket. As a schoolboy before he ran away to sea he wrote challenging a Surrey team at their ground at Mitcham, where Hobbs used to practice. You can imagine their chagrin when a team of young schoolboys marched in, having walked all the way from Carshalton as they could not afford the fare. Nevertheless they had a good day and Dad was given £5 for him and his team. Later as a young man he played against W. G. Grace in a charity match and bowled him out for a duck. The great man was not at all pleased. One other ability that always impressed us was the facility he had, that none of us inherited, of being able to add up four columns of figures at once.

He never lost his spirit. When he was seventy he had to have a leg amputated owing to circulatory trouble. We were told to expect the worst. Instead, as he came to, he said "You can throw that away—it's no more use to me" and proceeded to make a remarkably quick recovery—to the great surprise of the doctors and nursing staff. At seventy-five after intense pain he had to have the other leg amputated and lived beyond all medical expectation for a further five years. Although he was by now frail, his face remained young and cheerful and he was convinced he spoke the truth when, sitting in his wheelchair, he used to boast to visitors "Do you know I have never had a day's illness in my life?" Mother was ostensibly a gentle, quiet person, but she too had a pioneering spirit although it was necessarily restricted by the ties of bringing up a family. The seafaring life that Dad led had appealed to her own adventurous spirit and she took us on holidays abroad in the days when only the rich did this and leaving these shores an exciting adventure not dared by any of our friends or acquaintances. Turning out some old household account books we were amazed to find how pitifully small the family income was in those early days—just 30/- a week—for we never wanted for a thing. The fact was that mother was an excellent manager and had her priorities right, for Dad looked to her to steer the family ship. Although he was friendly and kind to us and good fun, with a soft spot for Babs who looked incredibly like mother's photograph's when she too was young, mother was the centre of his world and that never changed the whole of his life.

Mother told us that when she married she could not even boil an egg, for in those solid Victorian days there were always servants for domestic chores even in middle class households. Nevertheless she was a fine needlewoman and made all our clothes, even the boys suits, when they were young. I remember one beautiful dress I had when I was a child of which I was inordinately proud; it was shantung with an exquisitely embroidered top. Each year either the top or the bottom was replaced; this went on for years and meant that not only had I something that always fitted me as I grew, and something new and pretty to feel proud of, but that I had never really lost my favourite dress. With my brothers eleven and twelve years older than myself, no older sisters and Babs not yet born there was no question of cast-offs or hand-me-downs. Mother became an excellent cook and her pastry rose just like the modern commercials on television. We always had farm eggs and "best fresh butter" as I well remember seeing slapped up between wooden pats, as they did in those days. How she managed I do not know but looking back I think that it was her pioneering spirit. Nothing would daunt her. If they could not afford the sort of house she had been brought up in and liked for us, she would make do. And this did not mean accepting things as they were. Oh no! It meant knocking down walls, adding a room here and a bathroom there. Out with that high bay window and in with a low bay and french windows. Turn that coal cellar into a play room; out with the kitchen range and in with an open coal fire; install a billiard table for the boys. Although we lived in that one house for many years it seemed that we moved many times, it changed so often. We never knew what sort of place we were going to live in from one year to the next; it was most exciting. One feature of it was an enormous cupboard under the stairs that was unusual in that it had a window. This I made my secret playroom. With its many cables, pipes and meters it became for me alternately the bridge and the engine room of a ship and from here I could steer the house to faraway places or even to school if it were a wet day. It was in this house that Tom (always Willie to me, as his real name was William) made the huge bookcase from the built-in kitchen dresser that was at this moment heading westward ahead of us, for even in those early days our collection of books always exceeded their accommodation. Willie also had a large printing press in this cupboard under the stairs. He was gifted and brilliant in so many different ways and this press produced the accompanying literature and brochures for his multifarious activities. Later he was to train in Art Publishing and eventually he established his own Company in London.

It is of some significance and worth recording that years later when we were all grown up and finances improved we moved to a house that by comparison was quite luxurious, sporting among its features french windows, a garden with three lofty walnut trees and an en-tout-cas tennis court bordered by luscious pear trees. Mother set about improving this house too. Nothing could stop her; it was in the blood, this pioneering spirit. Nevertheless, wherever we lived it was Home with a capital H for mother had that rare quality of enhancing any place wherever she happened to be. I think that if we had lived in a tent, to us it would have seemed like coming home to a palace. It was not by anything that she said, although even when in her eighties she was still very witty, for in spite of all this spirited pioneering she was always a quiet, reserved lady. She seemed somehow to radiate a light and warmth so that any room she was in the sun seemed to be shining there. You knew as soon as you turned into the drive whether she was in or not. I think those who advocate crêches, and husbands sharing the care of babies, do not realise what basic need they are denying their children. Who knows what social misdemeanours, wayout behaviour, and ultimately criminal tendencies can be traced back not only to broken homes but to ones where there is only a part-time mum, not from necessity but often from choice?

Of course mother was rather special. As a child I remember feeling sorry for all the other children because they did not have her as their mother, and I naturally thought they would feel just as sorry for themselves because of their bad luck. As a consequence I went around being very kind to these unfortunate beings and would invite them home to tea so that they could share in my good fortune. Unwittingly I made a lot of little friends this way and as an extra bonus was invited to join their various churches just before the annual Sunday School outing so that I could go along with them. This was an early introduction to comparative religions, certainly to the comparative merits of their social activities if nothing else. I was of course very welcome at the homes of these young friends, but if their mothers could only have known that my solicitude for their offspring was due to these ladies' supposed inferiority, the warmth of their welcome might have chilled to say the least.

In case it is thought that this view of mother is rather biased it is a fact that all her life people, including children and adolescents, gravitated to her as to a magnet. Even when she was in her late seventies we have seen men leave some glamorous female's company to talk to her, entranced for hours, and she was always affectionally referred to by family and friends as "The Lady". She came from an artistically gifted family who could all play the piano, sing and paint before they ever had a lesson. One sister was so talented that she was being trained by an Italian singing master until she gave up this vocation to run away and get married to one of grandfather's employees. Mother could sing, was a talented actress and was always chosen to play the leading lady at the amateur theatricals held in the Public Hall; her most remembered roles being Elizabeth I and Britannia. These stayed in the memory, we suspect, principally because she was chosen to play these parts by the general vote of her contemporaries, thus endorsing the opinion of the producer. Photographs of her at the time reminded us of the young Ellen Terry and we often thought how well mother would have graced the West End stage. One of our favourite ways of teasing her was to say, after some particularly tedious visitor had left, "What the West End stage missed when you decided to get married!" for mother had the facility of making the most boring person feel clever and important and apparently was quite unaware that she was making any particular effort.

Most of the tales we heard about her were told to us by our aunts, her sisters, or Dad, for she never lived in the past and was the most reticent of people. Apart from her father, who died very suddenly when mother was fourteen, her Aunt Eliza was the biggest influence in her life. She was a Headmistress who ran her own Academy for Young Ladies, and was a very grand person indeed, as mid-Victorian photographs show. Mother spent all her holidays with her and was over-awed by the atmosphere of erudition and the good manners that were expected of her. Mother was fond of quoting Aunt Eliza or her friend the Vicar to us and one dictum that came down to us was that tea should be the colour of pale straw. The Vicar's contribution to the good life was that it was essential that the last thing one should do before retiring for the night was to blow one's nose!

It must have been from Aunt Eliza that mother inherited her great love of books, especially history and poetry, and in many ways this was passed on to us. When we were young there was hardly a church or historic building that we were not taken into in our travels and today we would not dream of passing a spot on the map denoting a Roman Encampment or barrow without stopping to explore, and no holiday would be complete without acquiring a small library on the history of the district. Books were the currency of our childhood and were given and asked for at Christmas, birthdays, and as a convalescent treat after measles, whooping cough and the like. The first book I ever read long before I went to school was *The Red Eric* by R. M. Ballantyne, about a little girl who went with her father on whaling expeditions in his boat to all parts of the world. In all I read it seven times and when the spine became torn with use I repaired it with panels of suede leather, embossing the title on the leather with a red hot needle. Unluckily it was lost during wartime moves, but most of the classics that we were given in our childhood and all the twentieth-century poets, beautifully printed on deckle edged paper in their first editions, had fortunately survived and would, we hoped, be pounding their way westward.

There would appear to be a strong matriarchal streak on mother's side of the family for many of the women folk seemed quite go-ahead for Victorian days. Another of her aunts was not only a music teacher but played professionally and gave concerts at Masonic and other gatherings. What most impressed us was the fact that she had someone to carry her music case so that her fingers should not be ruined for the performances. Three other aunts of mother's had a stage coach inn apiece in their own right, in what in those days would have been darkest Surrey. We did a tour once to see these hostelries, for mother had sometimes been invited to stay with these aunts. Elizabethan and timbered, these inns are there to this day, and although they are now fashionable and in the stockbroker belt, they have not really become spoilt. In fact they look picturesque still, for they are genuinely old. Her visits to them seemingly had no influence on mother, for she always preferred tea as a beverage—the colour of pale straw, of course.

It was not surprising therefore that mother put education very high up in her list of priorities for us. There were no family allowances or grants in those days and with farm eggs, best fresh butter and holidays abroad I do not know how she managed it, but I was sent to a private school. The main bill of fare was French, Music, Good Manners, Play-the Game and Long Live the British Empire! Curtseying was taught and was obligatory daily, presumably in case you should by chance run into one of the Royal Family. Academic standards were not high but a term or two at a tutor's bridged the gap to a school where they were very high indeed. In time Babs went to this private school, too, but as I left there when I was thirteen we were never there at the same time. I shall never forget that school or the friends I made there. Incredibly, six of us still keep in touch one with another. Ethel was a particular crony and together we wrote and produced plays, put on conjuring shows, initiated a Secret Society and wrote and published a magazine. This last, copies of which we laboriously copied out by hand in penny exercise books, was an astounding success, not for any literary merit, but for the fact that it rated a mention at morning prayers.

Not so much a mention as a hullabaloo for, sad to relate, our masterpiece was banned on the grounds that Bessie Bunter was not a suitable person for young ladies to read about. Needless to say we were bombarded by the rest of the school for under the counter copies and offered twice the asking price of 2d to boot. What an early lesson in salesmanship psychology we were unwittingly given! Ethel came to the island only a few months ago and so well were those early links of friendship forged that we automatically picked up the threads, as we always do, somewhere between the ages of six and twelve years at which latter age our close collaboration ended, due to Ethel and her family moving from the district.

I was given a good foundation in music there, both in the curriculum and as an extra, for the school was fortunate in having an excellent music teacher, Miss Madden, a young and enthusiastic mistress. It was due to her and mother's encouragement that I was able to study music and the piano seriously until well after the age of twenty. Mother bought me the magazine *Music and Youth* and when that came out it was always a red letter day. Willie bound the copies for me and he and I practised together—he the violin and I the piano. This particular partnership came to an abrupt end when I told him that he had played a wrong note. He flung the violin across the room and never played it again.

The next school must be mentioned because it was while I was there that an island influenced my whole career, and strange to relate, it was an island that never existed.

It came about in this way. The Headmistress, an austere and academic lady with lofty ideals which she tried by precept to instil into us, had banned a play that a friend and I planned to put on for Speech Day. My friend was the leader of the school orchestra and we were arranging music not only as an overture and during the intervals but as background at the more dramatic moments. The music was to be mostly Beethoven, Tchaikowsky, Brahms and some old Irish folk music—the play J. M. Synge's *Playboy of the Western World*. "Parents," said the Headmistress "would not approve of the play—there are too many dead bodies in it." Or words to that effect. We were really shattered. The play was well under way and we had spent weeks rehearsing it and arranging the music. We thought that everyone would be stunned with the poetry and sheer artistry of our epic production, and now it was to be banned just like the magazine at the last school. I felt like running away.

When therefore soon after this the Headmistress sent for me again I was in rebellious mood and prepared, with adolescent bravado, to "stand my ground" whatever the interview was to be about. She smiled kindly at me from her Olympian heights. "You have a brilliant future before you in History" she said to my great astonishment. "Next term you move up to the Sixth Form and you will then take a scholarship to Oxford. It will mean a great deal of hard work of course, and," she added "you will have to drop Geography." Drop Geography—Never! I thought grimly to my-self, unable to change from the tragic figure of a frustrated and misunder-stood artist in which I had cast myself to that of a future academic. My mind was in a whirl. While I stood there thoughts chased through my mind like streaks of lightning. Oxford! I doubt if the family could afford it even with a scholarship. I was not capable of winning one anyway. How flatter-ing, though, to think that anyone thought that I could, especially this august lady—even though she was still in my "hate" book. I did not want to become a bluestocking for at that period it was exceptional for girls to go to University unless, as it appeared to me, they were dull and brainy. I wanted, too, wider horizons than, as I thought, the narrow one of an aca-demic career. I planned in fact to be a journalist. All this went through my mind as I stood there. But above all, the transcending thought was that I did not want to "drop" Geography.

The reason for my reluctance was this. We had recently been given the project of choosing a spot on the map of the world, fixing its latitude and longitude, then describing in the detail the geography—flora, fauna, climate, physical aspects etc. This had been a rivetting occupation and did not seem like work at all. I had drawn a map of an imaginary island in the Indian Ocean showing rivers, mountains, coastline and vegetation, then described in much detail every possible aspect including population, occupations, produce, diet, the exports and imports and even a bit of supposed history thrown in. It was all so real I practically lived on that island. So I was looking forward to Geography in the Sixth with, I thought, similar fascinating projects in mind.

This I tried to explain to the Headmistress and blurted out that I wanted to carry on with both History *and* Geography. There was a bit of a fuss; an icy reception to my plea to do both, and warnings that the History would suffer and jeopardize my chances of gaining the scholarship. Eventually to my surprise she reluctantly agreed and said that she would arrange a curriculum for me. Maybe I had gained her sympathy because as it hap-pened Geography was her specialist subject.

71

So this island that never existed led us eventually to this one that did, for if I *had* followed that academic career planned for me it would have been strange indeed if the set of circumstances culminating in early retirement and the events that followed would have taken the course they did. For, sad to relate, this dual curriculum was destined to fail. In the first place Advanced Geography was a bitter disappointment. Instead of exploring the romance of faraway places the studies became all very technical dealing with isobars and contours, rainfall and atmospheric pressure. Relieved as I was to drop Latin in which I could only succeed, owing to a blindspot in grammar, in making Caesar lose all his battles instead of winning them, I now found I had a blindspot too in this aspect of Geography, whereby I had an unhappy knack of making rivers run uphill and isobars flow wildly in all directions. Added to which I found it all incredibly boring.

There was another thing. Willie was paying for me to have private tuition in shorthand as I had expressed a desire to learn this in readiness for my chosen career. Of course nothing as lowdown as shorthand, typing or any of the domestic sciences were allowed even to be mentioned at this school, so my shorthand was necessarily practised in secret. Fascinated by the sheer artistry of the whirls and scrolls I was learning I took all my History notes down in shorthand. Unfortunately history had become complicated as it embraced nineteenth-century European affairs, secret treaties, and all the intricate machinations of the politics of the period. I found to my horror that I had become so enamoured with producing beautiful flowing curves that I had taken in none of the content and I now found myself unable to read any of it back—and I dare not confess the reason why. Panic set in as I realised I would not be able to hand in work of the required standard. What with rivers running uphill on the one hand and European politics stirred into a seething ferment by the curves and hooks of Pitman's shorthand on the other it was a wonder that a cosmic disaster and a nineteenth-century world war of gargantuan proportions allowed anyone to enter the twentieth century at all.

Desperate measures were needed. Fortunately there was a way out. Sometimes the History and Geography lessons coincided and it was left to me to choose which one to attend. I now attended neither and played one off against the other by always supposedly producing homework on the other subject. Now and again I put in a brief appearance or produced a bit of written work to show that I was still a pupil at the school, but most times I found myself an empty classroom whenever I was due at either of these subjects and filled in the time reading and writing. Consequently my English Literature improved enormously. I won the Magazine prize and was made Editor of the School Magazine, but had very strange looks indeed from the History and Geography mistresses, the latter making me a special and public mention in her farewell speech when she left the school. I did wonder later if perhaps I drove her to go. Although I got certificates for shorthand and eventually some for speed I never made practical use of it nor ever had a job that required its use.

In due course Babs arrived on the scene and had reached the stage when I hoped that my school exercise books would help her in her scholastic career. My two brothers, who were already young men when I was a child, had helped and looked after me and, now that I had a young sister, I couldn't wait to do the same for her. Trevor, the younger of the two, had taught me to play chess at a very early age. He and I also played bezique before I was the age to go to school. He was incredibly handsome and great fun. There was a great rapport between him and Willie although they were so different. Willie was brilliant artistically and had the looks of a film star or West End actor and an alluring personality that drew everyone to him like a magnet, men women and children, especially women. They fell for him like nine-pins, yet he was completely unspoilt, had high ideals and burnt himself out in his endeavour to attain them. Trevor was the more studious one and I remember being very impressed by his library of books on differential calculus, trigonometry and the like, and the blueprints he produced as he studied engineering. He eventually qualified as an engineer and became a Chief Engineer at an extremely early age. Later we did photography together. Even after he was married we joined a Photographic Club in London and from our darkrooms in our respective homes would ring each other up sometimes at 3 a.m. to discuss a problem or compare notes on fixers and developers. Once we went on a photographic expedition to the Inner Temple on a raw spring day. Trevor caught a chill, pneumonia set in and within a week he was dead. His photographs were exhibited posthumously and one of these which I finished processing for him was awarded a prize at the Club Exhibition.

Photography had been an early love of mine. At the age of four years I had a frame with sensitized paper in it whereby by placing say a leaf or flower in it and exposing it to the sun for a few seconds you had a "photograph" of the subject. This was sheer magic and inspired me when I was ten or eleven years old to make my own camera from a cigar box. A photograph taken with it survived childhood and turned up a short time ago in a box of rather more sophisticated exhibition pictures.

Willie always took me under his wing. He organised my birthday and Christmas parties, putting on shows helped by Trevor, and distributing really handsome prizes to my young friends in some novel way such as having them fish for them over the top of a screen decorated to represent a tank while he and Trevor crouched behind hooking the presents on the lines. Willie designed and made fancy dresses from paper, card and wire for me and when he had painted designs on them they really looked quite stunning at the dancing class performances put on for parents and at other functions. He would even check my school clothes at the beginning of term and had a rubber stamp made with my name on it in italic script so that everything should be correctly marked.

He was a member of the Magic Circle, designed and constructed all his own tricks, printed beautiful brochures and gave performances at charity concerts, having me on stage as his assistant in some exotic garment, designed by him of course. As a hobby also he established an indoor cricket school in London planning everything himself from scratch. Many clubs were coached there by famous cricketers. He had me along there at the nets being bowled at by Wright the Kent bowler, coached in batting by a famous Yorkshire veteran, and for good measure by members of the Middlesex team and several other cricketers practising for the forthcoming test series. The Press got to hear about this and pictures appeared on the front pages of the Evening News and the Evening Standard. Dad of course was immensely proud of this, even more than the time a schoolfriend and I tramped the double journey of twenty-six miles on main roads to the Oval to see Jack Hobbs play in a Test match against Don Bradman.

When I left school Willie gave me a homily and warnings about the different kinds of people I would now meet and added injunctions not to be influenced by them. When he got married he even took me on his honeymoon with him and his bride—a situation that did not go down too well at first, even though I was only a schoolgirl. Nevertheless when once Molly, my sister-in-law, had got used to having a third person present on her honeymoon we became very close.

Willie always vetted my boy friends, and when Babs was born he took her under his wing, too. He wanted her to be named Roselyn and this she is, Babs being the pet name she has always been called as the baby of the family.

My school books only helped Babs for a very short time and soon she was way ahead on her own having made up her mind at an early age that she wanted to teach. This she did, training at Cambridge, and much to mother's delight eventually became a Headmistress, thereby keeping in the tradition of Aunt Eliza. Again, although we both went in for Amateur Dramatics Babs was the one who really kept on the family tradition by producing and acting in plays at Cambridge, later joining an Amateur Repertory Company and doing as many as five shows in a week-end all over the country, teaching Drama at Evening School and acting as Adjudicator at a County Festival.

This brief sketch of our early background and family history may explain to some extent why we were heading west into an unknown adventure. That we were middle-aged, single and therefore free to do so is explained by the fact that we were unwilling to break these close family ties. Both of us had broken off engagements in the past. Babs had only recently turned down persistent offers of marriage from her former Headmaster who, nevertheless, left her everything in his will stating that his dearest wish was that they should marry but as she could not see her way to agree to this, he left everything to her, his dearest friend.

Apart from our adventurous father and very special mother we had for many years these two handsome cricket loving brothers who were always at hand to do anything that we required. There was twenty years difference in age between Babs and them, and with me somewhere in the middle it was natural that they should have this protective attitude towards us both. This double bulwark against the stresses and strains of Life had not only given us an upbringing in a rarefied atmosphere, but in addition, an inbuilt predisposition to polyandry but not the moral latitude to go with it, or we might have broken with tradition and faced life with a brace of husbands apiece. Nevertheless I for one always found it necessary to have two boy friends at a time. This naturally led to complications, heart searchings and on one occasion to an almost insoluble situation when I found myself involved on a holiday on the continent with two such attachments who had only met for the first time on the boat train at Victoria Station. An emotional climax on top of a glacier in Switzerland of all places, where it was intended that I should become engaged to one, only led me helter skelter into the arms of the other in the valley below and to the conclusion that the marital state was not for me.

This attitude can best be summed up in a phrase coined at an exclusive little pre-wedding party in London, at which five of us consumed nine bottles of champagne in record time before the rest of the guests arrived. I run very well on champagne, at least I think I do, which really comes to the same thing. At about the half way mark when someone as usual was trying to marry me off, I waved my glass in the air and gave to the world the immortal couplet "The world is so full of lovely men, to choose just one is beyond my ken." It would have never have put Shakespeare out of business, but by full time we were all convinced it would.

Tragically we lost our marvellous brothers within five months of each other when they were thirty-nine. Our parents lived to a good age, Dad as has been mentioned, in spite of losing both legs, until nearly eighty, and mother still lovely and radiant to the last, surviving him until she was nearly eightyfive. It was our privilege to look after them both in their later years as they had looked after us when we were young, and now that we no longer had the fun of their companionship we were off to seek a little adventure of our own and fulfil our childish dreams.

So as we journeyed westward through the "darkening shires" our past was left behind; a past we left without regret for it had brought us to this momentous point in our lives and would be treasured always, sustaining us through any trials that we might meet.

Somewhere on the road ahead all our worldly possessions travelled too, containing our links with the past and our hopes for the future; a future which we sped through the starlit winter night to meet with mounting excitement.

Nos 1 and 2 Bassett Court

My first view of the island, from Wool Down

a

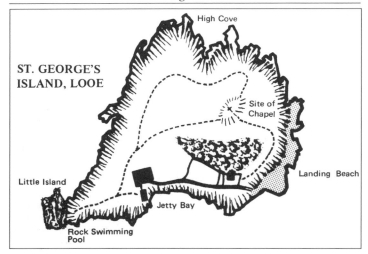

Map of The Island

A close-up from the air

b

Island House

Smugglers Cottage

Bridge across to 'Little Island'

Unloading fuel for the
generators

A willing helper

Babs meets a visitor

d

Chapter 5
Entry of supporting characters

The next afternoon as we eased down into Looe we were amazed to see the pantechnicon just a couple of hundred yards ahead of us and we crossed the bridge over the river to West Looe as though we had made the journey of some 240 miles in convoy.

Babs had written to pass the message on to Wren Toms that we should arrive in the late afternoon of December 22nd and would he please have his boat at the quay ready to take us over to the island. There was no sign of Wren Toms or his boat—just Alfy Martin and in no time at all it was pitch dark. Leaving Alfy to supervise the unloading into Nancollas's store on the quayside in the strict reverse order necessary we repaired to the cottage and eventually met up with Wren Toms.

Like a douch of cold water it hit us that late December is hardly the best time to move furniture in an open boat in darkness to an island that did not have a harbour. What sent our spirits plummetting however was when Wren Toms said that several journeys would have to be made and that they would have to be at the top of the spring tides. We were in utter despair at the thought of having to stay on the mainland until the Spring. In our ignorance of things maritime we thought that spring tides meant just that. If I had concentrated on those isobars and suchlike in my youth we would have known as Wren went on to explain that spring tides are especially high and come twice every month with the new moon and again with the full moon. They are exceptionally high at the vernal and autumnal equinox. Should they coincide with gales accompanied with rain, rivers burst their banks, flooding occurs and disaster overtakes vulnerable areas. It was this combination of circumstances that had caused the flooding in Looe on our first visit on that memorable night in late October the previous year. As I write we have just experienced the highest spring tides for 300 years due to an unusual conjunction of sun, moon and earth. Accompanied by gales of storm force they caused a disaster the telling of which must be kept for the future! Since coming to live on the Island we have learned to regulate our lives by the tides but at that time it was our first encounter with this natural phenomenon and we soon realised how our lives and future movements were hinged on its movements.

Relieved that we had only to wait until the next Spring tide due at the beginning of January we prepared to spend Christmas in the cottage. Once again Doug and Cecily came over from their visit to Devon to spend part of the holiday with us. They were both anxious to join us in our island life. Much as we would have liked to have them, for Doug was one of those chaps who could put his hand to anything, we felt that initially we could not take on the extra financial burden that their help would have entailed. With their three children there were five of them. The only certain income was Babs, greatly reduced with her new appointment, and my pension. No work or market gardening had been done on the island for six months, and it was uncertain what income, if any, there would be from the daffodils the first year. What was certain was that there would be quite a strain on our finances putting everything in order after six months neglect. We would without doubt have to pay for labour, specialised and boatwise, and we quite frankly quaked at the thought of having to feed the seven of us, keep three homes going, run a boat and a car in addition, not forgetting the fact conveniently overlooked by others that as single people we are taxed up to the hilt, and I have never enjoyed equal pay although most expenses naturally are equal. We felt we had enough on our plate and that was the understatement of the year. We told them regretfully that we must settle in first and if it appeared a feasible proposition they could join us later. With the promise that they could spend a holiday with us in the early summer we sped them on their way.

It seemed hardly credible that it was just fourteen months ago that we had come on that hurriedly planned and brief visit looking for a holiday cottage and now here we were poised to take off for an entirely new life on an island, and in mid winter too. Not that that worried us—our only concern was these spring tides which we awaited with much impatience. We filled in the time (only, in fact, a matter of days for they were due on January 2nd) by buying more "protective clothing" and a couple of outboard motors.

Of the three boats that belonged to the island, *The Islander*—an eighteen foot 6 h.p. diesel motor boat, a twelve foot metal sailing boat, and an eight foot fibre glass dinghy, two were in the harbour—*The Islander* and the dinghy. Miss Whitehouse who used to live with her parents on the island but later moved to the mainland to run a goose farm, had been rowing over to the island in the dinghy when the weather was suitable to put out dried food for the cat who would not leave. Wren Toms had commandeered some help and had been going out to the island to put *The Islander* in order, for owing to Mr Whitehouse's ill-health it had not been used for some time. One of these helpers was a massive man called Mac, a Chief Bosun on shore leave. He was also to help with the moves to the island and solved our immediate labour problems as he was willing to come over to the island and work on a day-to-day basis until his leave expired. Judging by his muscle, size and experience of the sea we reckoned he would be a great asset and just the kind of casual labour that would suit us.

At last it was Friday January 1st and we awaited the magic spring tides due together with Wren's week-end—for he worked for the Council during the week—on the next day, Saturday, but with them came strong winds and high seas. Mac called on Friday to say that the sea was "making up", that it was coming in from the west and back washing round the island. Landing the next day Saturday, he said, would be impossible. Seeing our obvious and bitter disappointment and to convince us that it was impossible he offered to take us out in *The Islander* to see for ourselves.

Babs decided not to come as she had a touch of bronchitis and was still rather chesty, so just Mac and I set sail. It was a wild winter's day. As soon as we left the harbour we could see high seas breaking over the Rannies, a reef of rocks extending from the furthermost south-eastern tip of the island, and there was nothing to be seen on the jagged horizon but white horses riding wildly towards us. Breakers surged all round the island and were smashing on the rocks at Hannafore. We rode giddily over mountainous rollers and as we approached what should have been the landing beach there was no beach to be seen at all; just a wall of shingle and seaweed thrown up by the surf and a foaming sea cascading over the rocks. The island looked as though it would subside under the pounding onslaught and inwardly I wondered if there would be any island left for us to live on. As we sailed westward past the island towards the wild sunset great Atlantic rollers loomed above us and our sturdy little boat bravely climbed up and up before plunging into the troughs on the other side. When Mac was satisfied that I was convinced that landing would be impossible we turned back. He need not have worried; I was certain that no one would be able to land ever again, and that we might as well have bought a planet in outer space for all the use the island would be to us as a future home.

All this time Babs was watching from Hannafore, and thinking how lonely and vulnerable our little boat looked in that stormy expanse of ocean for not another craft was to be seen. She was convinced she would never see us again.

Back on dry land in spite of her fears, we decided to console ourselves instead with a shopping expedition to Plymouth the next day. As though we had not enough books to take with us we added to our store by buying more, but mostly they were on fruit and vegetable growing and astronomy. We did not stay long. Back in West Looe an eerie sight caught my eye as we drove along the quayside. Our fibre glass dinghy was lying on the quayside and attached to its upturned side was a hand, just a hand, nothing more. Horrified, we skidded to a halt and tumbled out of the car. Our fears were soon stilled however when investigation showed Wren Toms aboard his own boat the *Orlando* below as the tide was out, and just about to give himself a heave up by grasping the dinghy.

"Come aboard!" he invited hospitably, extending the hand to us to help us down the vertical iron ladder into his boat. We stayed for at least an hour while he ground in new valves into his auxiliary engine. Lovingly he held up a valve or a gasket and proceeded to explain patiently and in great detail exactly what he was doing. It may not have seemed so strange to Babs who, after all, was a car driver and presumably knew the names at least of things that lived under the bonnet of the car, but to me it was all like black magic. This was the first time I had seen a gasket. I remember once on a drive in the country a strange knocking developed in the car and Babs said, "That's the gasket gone." I wanted to go back and look for it and could never understand why we did not and why we had to put up with the knocking until we found a garage. All the time Wren was explaining what he was doing an absurd jingle kept going through my head,
A-Tisket, A-Tasket, at last I've seen A-Gasket!"
Even so it did look to me rather like a glorified washer. Little did I know how closely bound up with gaskets and all their relations my future life would be.

To our delight it transpired that all these preparations were for making a foray over to the island with some of the furniture the next day, Sunday. Wren did say casually that Mac was not too keen. We could quite understand why.

Wren then made an idle remark that convinced us that MI5 had emigrated to Looe. "Mac told me that you had been to Plymouth," he said. We had not told anyone nor had we seen anyone en route. In fact our destination had been one of those spur of the moment decisions when once we were on our way. Furthermore we had been gone so short a time that the only way people in Looe could know was if we had been spotted in Plymouth and someone had telephoned the news through to Looe, and we didn't think that we rated that hot a line. Walking back to the cottage everyone we met asked us if we had enjoyed our trip to Plymouth and when one of them was Mac we asked how he knew. "Oh! Nancollas told me," he said. Sometime later we spoke to Mr Nancollas about this. "Yes! I did hear you were in Plymouth," he said non-commitedly. And there the matter ended—unresolved. It was the first but not to be the last of our experiences of the mysterious workings of the grape-vine.

High tide on Sunday, January 3rd was at the uninviting hour of 5.58 a.m. so we set the alarm for 5 a.m. It was an icy cold morning and more like the middle of the night. I donned two of everything, slacks over jeans, two thick fisherman's jerseys, seaman's stockings over socks, sea boots, woolly hat, anorak and string gloves. Mac called at 5.45 still very doubtful about the advisability of trying at all. It was pitch dark and bitingly cold.

He and Babs went round to Hannafore by car to inspect the state of the sea for Mac was convinced that this would show that an attempt would be out of the question and most foolhardy. While they were gone Wren Toms arrived and announced cheerfully, "All set fair to go." I must say his manner and appearance inspired confidence. Aged about 27 he was a tall, strong, handsome young man. He wore thigh sea boots topped by a red shirt and with his black curly hair and vivid blue eyes he made a striking figure. He looked like a swashbuckling but friendly pirate, ready to dare anything. He was aptly named Wren for his eyes were and are always twinkling, and bright with optimism. You somehow felt that if he said we were to set sail in a sieve you would go quite happily. The tale was that he used to play truant from school to be with the boats. As we came to know him we thought that if this were so it was time well spent, for there was apparently nothing that he did not know about the sea and boats. He has an uncanny knack of knowing exactly the right thing to do with any nautical problem. Some say he takes risks and he probably does, but they are calculated risks based on experience and one felt that he would not put his boat and his life in danger foolishly.

The others returned to say that the sea even in the darkness could be seen creaming round the island. Wren however was already back in the

Orlando preparing to sail.

The great loading up from Nancollas's store now began. The refrigerator and deep freeze were trundled along the quayside like skittles by the burly Mac who had shoulders like an armchair. Just as smartly they were trundled back at Wren's command, "I want all the tea chests first." There were, as we knew only too well, thirty of these and as they were full of books they had been stowed at the back of the store for the final trip, when the bookcases would hopefully be on the island waiting to accommodate them. To our horror the store now became a wreck as the unfortunate Mac had to clamber over furniture, clawing his way to the back and heaving and shoving as he tried to extricate the chests. We heard more than one ominous scrunch and hoped that a precious antique had not splintered under the onslaught or, worse still, that Mac had not cracked one of his bones. Much to our relief he still looked in one piece, and as happy as he could reasonably be expected to be, when he finally emerged and heaved the last of the chests onto the quayside.

These loaded up, Wren then allowed other items to follow. These were more or less hurled aboard willy-nilly as Wren was in a hurry and time was getting short with the tide dropping fast. We tried to see that a few useful items like a kettle and some pots and pans were thrown in but it was a chancy business.

During the chaos dawn broke, Venus shone brightly over the sea in the east, the tide went down rapidly and the vicar passed on his way to early morning service. He stopped to greet us and we were greatly comforted for we felt that we could do with his blessing. Babs and I then dashed back to the cottage to make fresh flasks of coffee while Wren roped up. We flung a few more things on board in passing and I hurriedly took photos of the poor *Orlando*. Weighed down and low in the water and piled high with an assortment of our belongings she had lost her beautiful lines and looked like some gigantic sea monster, distorted with pain and about to subside into a watery grave.

The tide was dropping fast. It was as though a plug had been taken out and Wren, having loaded and made fast everything to his satisfaction, was anxious to get away. Leaving the wreckage in Nancollas's store we slithered down the vertical iron ladder as best we could, tumbled into the boat, clambered over the piles of packing cases, pots and pans and the like to the only bit of shelter on the boat, the wheelhouse—a kind of half open cabin housing the steering and engine area. There was just room for the four of us to huddle together and by a judicious readjustment of elbows just enough clearance for Wren to steer.

Slowly the overburdened *Orlando* moved towards the harbour mouth. Once out of its protection a wild scene confronted us. A wracking sea raced across our bows. The *Orlando* bucked as cross waves broke over the deck and wheelhouse and spray whistled past overhead. A corkscrew motion then began to develop. Hemmed in by packing cases in the rear and unable to see through the streaming glass of the wheelhouse before us we clung to each other and anything we could lay our hands on to prevent ourselves from falling on to Wren, who was having to hold hard to keep the boat on course, and, for all we knew, afloat. The cargo began to creak and move ominously as the *Orlando* twisted and writhed and crashed down with a grinding thump. I thought we were hitting the seabed every time we plunged down through the boiling surf with a sickmaking jolting thud. We were in fact "crossing the bar". This is a bar of water that develops in silted up tidal river mouths when the sea is running, in the case of Looe anyway, in an easterly or south-easterly direction or any direction if the seas are strong enough. The outgoing tide from the river meets the incoming waves with most spectacular results. The effect is a series of criss-cross chopping and swift running waves that pile on each other so fast it is impossible to ride them. The resulting maelstrom is worsened if the outgoing river is swollen with rain and sea it meets is rough. It can be quite catastrophic. Add a gale and the maelstrom becomes a mountainous frenzy. With the wind in the wrong direction even with just a fair tide running a small boat can be whisked right round so that it faces the way it was coming. This was something that we did experience later in our adventures. Luckily for our peace of mind at this time we knew nothing of the bar and its evil possibilities; we only knew we were in rough and unmanageable seas.

Wren's eyes glittered with excitement, and such was the confidence he inspired that although this really was a nightmarish journey I cannot remember that we were unduly worried even when, at the end of one particularly unnerving crash and twisting jolt, Wren said as he clung to the wheel, "I didn't expect the bar to be as bad as this; it is the worst trip I have ever had!". Memory does not record any reaction or comment from Mac. No doubt like us he was clinging on for dear life to anything that was handy. We like to think that diplomacy restrained him from voicing any opinion. We have often wondered since what the local boatmen thought of this mad expedition, for not even the fishing fleet ventured out for days in that wild sea in midwinter, let alone a boat the size of the *Orlando*, weighed down as she was with a heavy cargo. We realise now that no one but Wren would have attempted it.

Thankfully as we approached the island, we saw that some of the landing beach was still there and in the shelter of the western rocks exposed by the outgoing tide it was relatively calm. Wren took the *Orlando* as close as he could without going aground. We were to go ashore in his dinghy which he had towed behind and had somehow survived the battering. It was not an easy operation to climb over the side and heave oneself into the bouncing dinghy with no ladder or rope to help. I had brought my precious new Pentax camera with me and had clung to it throughout the hazardous journey. I now handed this to Wren for safety and with Mac below to catch me, if need be, I managed to decant myself into the dinghy. What I had not realised was that Wren would not be coming ashore at this stage. He was to wait on board and steady the *Orlando* upright with wooden legs as the tide ran out and left her high and dry. He would then be able to unload onto dry land. When the tide came in again in the afternoon and refloated her we would return to the mainland. So when Babs descended after me into the dinghy Wren handed the camera to her. Mac now rowed the dinghy on to the beach and helped me ashore. Babs stood up to follow, but Mac, without looking back, got hold of the rope and gave the dinghy a tremendous heave to lift it out of the water on to dry land. The sudden and unexpected lurch took the boat from under Babs' feet and sent her head over heels backwards over the stern into the sea. She was completely submerged in the water, Pentax and all. She was gasping as we rushed to pull her out. She had swallowed a good bit of sea water and was a bit shocked but apart from being sopping wet appeared to be otherwise unharmed. We rushed her up to the house and lit a fire of sorts for as she had not got over the touch of bronchitis we did not think a ducking in the icy sea of a January dawn would do her much good. It was now that my wearing two of everything came in very useful. I simply peeled off one layer and soon Babs was dry clad. I dare not look at my beautiful new Pentax. I feared it would be completely ruined. There was nothing I could do about it anyway until I was back on the mainland.

The caterpillar tractor which we had acquired along with other farming equipment with the island now came into its own. This would ride over shingle whereas anything with wheels would sink in and become bogged down. The versatile Wren got this going and soon he and Mac trailed up the first load of packing cases. One of these was the "ditty box" full of photographic equipment and to our great delight we found a bottle of dry sherry among the bottles of chemicals. This fortified us all while Babs and I made drinking chocolate to have with our cheese sandwiches. We did not unpack the books as we had nowhere to put them and as the darkroom had not yet been allocated there seemed no point in unpacking that either, especially as no more sherry had come to light. Wren and Mac stowed all the cases in the farmhouse kitchen which now began to look like a smugglers' den or a pirates' hide-out. No sooner were they all up from the beach when Wren said we should have to leave at once to catch the tide. This time fortunately we climbed into the *Orlando* while she was still aground on her legs, and waited until Wren could float her off. While doing so we pondered on the fact that a collection of hundreds of books and some photographic equipment was hardly enough to set up home on an uninhabited island. Nevertheless it was a start and the expedition was a novel way to spend a Sunday to say the least.

We reached harbour without incident for the bar had subsided somewhat with the incoming tide and riding with it instead of against it we were soon safely moored up alongside the quay. Ethrelda, an old Cornish lady with whom we had become friendly and who had been Toby-sitting for us made up a cup of tea, and snug and warm we told her the tales of the day. Babs so far felt no ill effects from her ducking in the sea, but I had not enough courage yet to inspect the camera too closely except to mop it as dry as I could.

The next day I felt very tired and stiff and wondered if perhaps I was not young or fit enough for this island lark. After food, drink and a visit to the hairdresser's however the sap rose once more and everything again seemed possible and exciting. Mrs Mac, on the other hand, called round to say that Mac was full of cold and sneezes and had gone off to be X-rayed. This seemed a dramatic outcome to yesterday's events and we thought at once of the ominous scrunchings we had heard in Nancollas's store. We were more than relieved to hear that the X-ray examination had been pre-arranged and had no connection with our expedition.

The Whitehouses, who were temporarily living in Looe, had invited us round to tea and for the second time we had experience of the mysterious powers of the grapevine; not only mysterious but inventive to an incredible degree. Not only did Mr and Mrs Whitehouse know everything in great detail of the happenings of the previous day, and this we quite under-stood for all the inhabitants of Hannafore would have had a grandstand view of the voyage of the *Orlando*, but they knew of conversations behind closed doors that had never taken place. One tale they repeated to us left us open mouthed with astonishment. Mr Whitehouse had been told that a member of the B.B.C. had taped a conversation with the Misses Atkins and that it was being held for safe keeping in the offices of a West Country newspaper. The informant of the informant (never identified), swore he had seen it there himself. Why for safe keeping? we asked ourselves hys-terically afterwards. Had we been bugged as suspects in the pay of the Russians? Was it thought that we had bought the island at their expense to set up a hidden submarine base or perhaps secretly land them at dead of night to install a nuclear bombsite trained on the Naval base at Devonport? At our trial the tape would be produced with a triumphant flourish and we would be marched off to the Tower of London while the West Country paper would make the scoop of the century! Perhaps even writing these words will trigger off a set of explosive laden rumours and if we are not careful we *shall* be marched off to the Tower "pending enquiries".

Once again this mystery was never resolved, and it was only the first of many quite unfounded rumours that dog us to this day. A favourite old annual is that the island is up for sale. Every year without fail someone will step ashore and say "I hear the island is up for sale." What baffles us is the amount of minute detail that accompanies these quite unfounded rumours. Not only are we given the name of the purchaser, but the amount he is paying, sometimes his address and, usually, where we are going to live after the sale. I must say they are up to date in one respect; the ru-mours always take into account inflation and each year the amount for which we have clinched the deal goes up. Our stock answer now is "Yes it *was* up for sale—ten years ago—and we are the ones who bought it."

The next spring tides would of course be in two weeks' time but Wren thought that if the weather were suitable we might make a short trip the following week-end when he would again be free. The neap tides due then would make a big unloading out of the question.

Meantime Babs made preparations for her first day at school and we tried to plan our future. It was now quite obvious that Babs would have to live in the cottage on the mainland and only come out to the island at weekends and holidays, and now that we had had a taste of winter seas we realised that even weekends would be out of the question except rarely in winter time. There was a great deal of work to do on the island just to keep it going and if we intended to carry on with the market gardening and the daffodil farm we should need labour. The question was whether the income from the produce was worth the cost of labour and sea transport and the worry involved. Hosts of friends were all set to come and help during their holidays, but even though many had long school or university vacations the help would naturally be sporadic. Wren was willing to come and work for us at week-ends and for a time Mac would be available full-time. This latter hope was knocked on the head however when Mrs Mac came round again to say that Mac's X-rays had shown a thrombotic condition and work of any kind would be out of the question for some time. We went straightway to visit him. There was poor Mac propped up in a made-up bed downstairs to save him climbing. He was coughing and sneezing with streaming eyes and we felt rather guilty; not that we knew beforehand that he was under the doctor, for he looked so big and strong one could not have suspected that he had a heart condition.

As for our future, we decided to play it by ear. Our main ambition, apart from an overwhelming desire to live on an island, was to make crafts, for, as well as the setting up of the pottery, Babs was very keen on all kind of crafts, as indeed we both were.

Not for the first time we now experienced the great kindness of the Cornish people. We had been told before coming down here that the Cornish resented the intrusion of strangers—up country people, as all those who come from the other side of the Tamar river, the natural boundary that practically cuts Cornwall off from the rest of the country, are called. If this is true, and in some cases it may justifiably be so then it is an attitude that one quickly has sympathy for and can appreciate. A picturesque folk of great natural charm, the Cornish have over the centuries had to battle with the elements in all the fury that the Atlantic can hurl at them, to make a precarious and often dangerous living from fishing, farming, and in the past, tin-mining. With the advent of train, coach and car the tourist industry was born, but—and this is a most significant "but"—the tourist trade at its height lasts for but four months of the year and again is dependent on the elements. Given a wet season many visitors who would otherwise come to the West Country do not come or, once arrived, flock home in their thousands. How many urban and city folk would like to have an inflated income for one-third of their working life each year, and have to live and bring up their families on little or no other income for the other two-thirds

87

of the year? Who would not resent "foreigners" who come to take the pickings of the tourist trade from a people who at last have been able to supplement their hard won earnings? Not that it is always the case. If people, for love of Cornwall, come here to earn an honest living and do not try to oust the locals or snatch their living from them, are not "uppity" nor think they can run the affairs of the Cornish for them better than they can themselves, they will find there are no finer friends than the Cornish. Many are welcomed and helped as we ourselves were. In any case we had not come to make a living. With Babs' salary and my pension we aimed only to live on the island and be self-sufficient financially, but how to do it with Babs having to work on the mainland was the rub now that Mac had been forced to opt out. Many of the folk we met in Looe were very concerned on our behalf.

At this time the Tyler family in particular took us under their wing. Although from East Looe originally, Zena and Peter lived just opposite from us in West Looe. One night during one of our previous visits to the cottages I had acquired from one of Nancollas's auction sales, through the good services of Alfy Martin, a chest of drawers for 10/–. Close examination showed that under its five or six coats of paint was a fine naval chest with brass handles; each drawer had been inscribed by the carpenter *Lieutenant (Electrical)*, and had stops so that the drawers would not fly out with the movement of the ship in heavy seas. Delighted with my bargain I had it out in the courtyard one night and, with the recently acquired Black and Decker and its sanding attachment, succeeded at long last in stripping off all the coats of paint to reveal the mahogany beneath. By the time I had finished, the night was well advanced, but I was so engrossed that I was hardly aware of the passage of time or the banshee-like wailings that shrieked around the courtyard from the power tool. Next morning as I was lovingly smoothing the chest down with fine sandpaper by hand a rich Cornish voice from behind me called "Good morning! I do not want to appear curious but *would* you mind very much telling me what you were doing last night. I should *love* to know." And that was how we first met Zena. From then on she was a constant visitor and many times we were invited over for tea or coffee. We, in fact, saw the New Year in with them on the eve of our now famous journey over to the island in the *Orlando* with the crates of books.

On one occasion Zena gave me a demonstration of how to make a traditional Cornish pasty. I took colour pictures of the process on the

Mamiyaflex and tried out my new tape recorder by recording her instructions, given in her lilting brogue. Serving pasties to some of our special visitors and revealing the secret of the Cornish way of making them has now become part of the ritual of our entertainment, accompanied, of course, by home-made island wine.

From the very beginning the Whitehouses had been concerned about how we would manage on the island. "Who will collect your driftwood and who will transport your diesel oil?" had been but two of many doubts these good folk had expressed on our behalf. Others, including Zena, joined in with their fears about how we should cope with the generator, and Zena was particularly concerned when Mac had to drop out, for he was her father-in-law and she reckoned he would never be in a fit state to help us. One day she came over with the news that her son Charles would help at weekends when he was home from school and that his friend Duncan was also very keen to help. Duncan apparently had been brought up on a farm and knew all about tractors, generators and the like. That very same evening Charles and Duncan came over and tried out our newly acquired outboard engines in the courtyard. The ensuing noise resounding round the courtyard and reverberating throughout West Looe made it sound as though something nasty was going on at a racing car circuit nearby. Later they decided to take the motors round to Hannafore to try as they were afraid that the thunderous roar echoing round the courtyard would break all the windows in the neighbourhood. Very thoughtful we thought for ones so young. It was not until many moons later that we learned that outboard engines are water cooled and should only be run if certain parts are submerged in water, their natural habitat when in use. Nevertheless they gave us very good service until they were lost in the great storms and tides of 1974.

Mr and Mrs Whitehouse were still very perturbed about our lack of labour on the island and thought that two schoolboys coming in their free time at weekends was hardly sufficient for the day to day running of the island. These problems we pushed firmly ahead into the future. Our priority, and the only problem that bothered us was actually getting ourselves and all out furniture on to the island; that hurdle overcome we would then be free to tackle these, to our minds, minor snags.

Meantime there were numerous comings and goings to the cottage, with many visitors offering us advice and telling us what we should do. One of these callers was from the Ministry of Agriculture. There was, he said, a plague of starlings on the island and we should have to do something about if we did not want everything poisoned by their pollution. Years ago, he said, the woods there were completely destroyed by the starlings. Farmers dealt with the problem by letting off at them with a shot gun. Although I was a "shot" it had been strictly target shooting, and I reckoned I would not have the time and certainly not the inclination to go shooting at wild life, however much of a pest. As an alternative he recommended rockets which are set to go off automatically at intervals, the explosions frightening them off every time they returned, as they surely would. As these rockets were quite expensive we decided to shelve this problem along with all the others and deal with it when we came face to face with this particular menace.

Another visitor was Ethrelda who not only was our Toby sitter, and tidied and polished the cottage for us, but she was a welcome visitor socially as we were close to her cottage a few steps up Hannafore Lane. She particularly enjoyed hearing some of my tape recordings. The machine fascinated her and nothing gave her greater pleasure than to give recitations or read old Cornish tales in dialect into the microphone and to hear her efforts replayed. She was an excellent natural performer and had recited at many concerts. Alas! she is no longer with us but her tapes recall those happy evenings and her spirited encouragement of our island project. Doubting Thomases there may have been but this dear old lady was not one of them. "You are walking into the lion's mouth," she said, "but you will find your way through. You two are the kind who will succeed there, and you will—I know you will." She was a member of the Darby and Joan Club and she invited us round one evening to entertain the members with some of the recordings and to meet Mrs Skuse, the organiser, who was also a member of the Field Study Group, a fact that Ethrelda thought might interest us. There were two repercussions from this visit one of which echoes to this day and the significance of which will be told in due course. The other and more pertinent one at the time was an invitation from Mrs Skuse, a charming lady, to go to the next meeting of the Field Study Group and meet Dr Turk, a distinguished ornithologist.

A few days later we did this and it was arranged that the group should come over to the island in the summer and do a survey of all the natural life. We were thrilled about this as we were most anxious to learn all we could about our new "country" and hoped that in due course we should have experts in their different spheres to visit us. This was a good beginning.

We had also become acquainted with Miss Kempster and Miss Hoyle, both retired teachers, who had invited us round to tea. They suggested that we might like to go to a meeting of the Old Cornwall Society as their guests. As the next meeting was on Saturday we were delighted to attend and took Ethrelda, who was also a member. We found the talk given that evening most interesting as it was given by a lady, a representative of the Ministry of Works as it was then still called, the subject being "Excavations in the Isles of Scilly". We were introduced to a number of people, who, experts in their own field or amateur enthusiasts, were just the kind of people who could give us the information we wanted so much about the history, natural, archaeological and otherwise of our island, which we already knew had a fascinating history from early times. We joined the society there and then and expressed the hope that sometime in the future they would care to visit us as one of their projects.

Earlier in the day we had run into Mr Nancollas who invited us into *The Harbour Moon*, the sparking off point for our adventure just over a year ago, for drinks. Mr Nancollas was most enthusiastic about our plans and had many suggestions of his own. As chairman of the council (a position since superseded by the current upheavel and reorganisation of local government by that of mayor) he was keen to help. No doubt he was relieved that developers or a holiday camp had not acquired the island. Although we only knew for a fact that the West End actors had been after the island, rumours persisted that a famous holiday camp was keenly in the running. He had, he said, a farmer and his son who would come over and plough the land. He suggested that we might keep goats to keep the grass down. This latter seemed to us an admirable idea, especially as it conjured up visions of goats' milk, cheese, butter and yoghurt and we filed it in our minds as one of the more feasible suggestions that had been hurled at us from all sides.

We had now been resident in Looe just a fortnight and it seemed incredible that in that short time there should have been such a fever of activity and meetings up with so many people. Of course our advent was highlighted by the fact that it happened in the depth of winter in a Cornish fishing village and holiday centre. If we had come in August everyone would have been too busy, no doubt, except to notice in passing that the island had changed hands.

Wren's plan for a small trip to the island on Sunday was out of the question for the day dawned wet and windy. A walk up Hannafore Lane over to Hannafore, a walk that Toby declined, revealed a rough sea running in from the west accompanied with slashing rain. A walk along the beach to Wallace Quay, a quay in name only for all that was to be seen were but parts of a broken and partly submerged sea wall of long ago, was wet and extremely unpleasant. The island receding into a pall of mist temporarily lost its bright allure, but not its fascination, and the warmth of a coal fire in Bassett Court beckoned us back to its comfort. Poor Toby who was in his fourteenth year was suffering from "the screws", so to alleviate his pain we administered some aspirin.

All our hopes were now pinned on good weather for the following week-end when the spring tides were again due. The intervening days were not without incident. The first was a letter from a girl called Ruth. Her parents ran a smallholding up at Shutta, where Babs had had to reverse on that pitch-dark night on our first stay in Looe, and Ruth, recently back from working in the U.S., offered her services to us until her parents required her help in the growing season around May. In July she was to start training to become a probation officer. She called round to see us and was very keen to live on the island to help us for the next few months and was willing to come just for the cost of her insurance stamp and her board and lodging. However we persuaded her to accept £3 a week so that she would have some pocket money and, that fixed, she went off to straighten up her affairs. This seemed a very good arrangement to us. It would keep all the good folk quiet who were worrying about how we should manage, in particular about my being on the island alone, and it would give us a bit of breathing space to find our bearings without the commitment of permanent help and the financial liability it could become.

Secondly, Babs had now taken up her new appointment and was involved during the daytime in getting *her* bearings. The third incident caused us a bit more concern. Mr Nancollas called round to say that he was disappointed that Wren had been unable to make a trip over to the island at the weekend as he needed the store for his next sale and would-be vendors had nowhere to put their articles for sale. He therefore was arranging for one of the fishermen, (who, being self-employed, was freelance and therefore free, if necessary, during the week,) to move the furniture the very next day. Well, this was fine, but we did not think that Wren would be pleased. Having taken on the assignment, hazardous though it was, he would not willingly give it up. In fact, as we came to know him better, we realised that he had accepted it as a challenge with relish and it had become the breath of life to him. Luckily or unluckily depending whether you were Wren or Mr Nancollas the problem was resolved by the weather remaining wet and windy all week.

We knew that Wren would make an all out effort at the weekend for not only was it spring tides when he could make a major embarkation but if he missed yet another week-end someone else would be moving our furniture out. Looking back we know now that fishermen would not exactly be vying with each other for the privilege of getting their boats bashed to bits on our rocks. Only recently a small fishing boat sank off the rocks and it was fortunate that I was around at break of dawn on a late winter's morning to dispense dry clothing and cups of hot coffee to some local men, who, though not fishermen by occupation, had lived in Looe all their lives and knew every inch of the coastline. We knew therefore that we might be in for an even more hazardous trip and were perhaps slightly relieved when by Friday the gales had not abated, but more than apprehensive when Wren made an assignment for 4.30 a.m. on the Saturday to size up the possibilities sea-wise.

Our resolve was further weakened by the fact that we did not get to bed until 2 a.m. due to a series of visitors, all of whom had their own ideas on how we should cope with the problems of running an island. One man in particular, and I cannot recall how we became acquainted, was full of the idea that we should install yet another generator; that the diesel oil for it should be piped over from tankers on the mainland and everything else should be transported by helicopter. "Only £25 an hour" he said lightly. Not for the first time we wondered if we were the first human begins who intended to live permanently on the island. If all these schemes that were dinned into our ears at intervals were so wonderful why had not previous owners, many of whom had been monied people, adopted them? We know the answer now. Ever ready to pick up a crumb of knowledge and by our upbringing polite by nature, we listen.

We are still surprised by the number of "experts" who march onto the island and tell us exactly how to run the island and point out the grave mistakes we are making in varying activities—even though not one of them has ever coped with life on an island or has been professionally involved in any of the spheres about which they claim an expert knowledge. The professionals are, we find, much more diffident at handing out advice. Nevertheless we always listen when we hear what is almost an Island Litany: "You know, what you ought to do is . . ." even though it is

93

something we have tried and discarded years ago as impractical. We continue to hope that we shall pick up a pearl of wisdom. Babs is much more tolerant of unsolicited and often foolish advice than I am. If I am tired or have had to cope with a lot of stupidity and the well-worn opening phrase is aimed at me I sometimes "up and at 'em" and tell them exactly why we do not keep cows, sheep, geese, rabbits, deer, peacocks or what have you. It is almost worth the expenditure of adrenalin to see the look of stupified surprise on the faces of our amateur counsellors.

At this stage in our island saga we were avid listeners thirsting for knowledge, and, bedazzled by these grandiose schemes, rolled into bed unable to sleep for excitement even at 2 a.m. The time of high tide—4.30 a.m.—did not, therefore, seem a highly desirable time to arise in mid-January to face a sea journey in a more or less open boat. Promptly on the half hour Wren called and while I sank back thankfully into bed the luckless Babs drove Wren round to Hannafore to look at the state of the sea. Tremendous seas were running and Wren regretfully decided it was too rough to transport furniture. He suggested instead that the three of us drive into Plymouth to Clode's, the ship's chandlers on the Barbican, and buy some chain for the *Islander's* mooring buoy. He was to call for us at 9 a.m. Even before that still tender time of day, when it was scarcely daylight, our little cottage seethed with comings and goings. First Charles and Duncan arrived nautically booted and spurred, all set for a trip to the island, and they were bitterly disappointed that it was too rough. They were followed smartly by Zena, not, as one might expect, anxious about her offspring embarking on some foolhardy and dangerous expedition, but keen to join the entourage herself.

Ruth, her appetite whetted, also turned up to see what the chances were of coming over to the island. As she was a Roman Catholic and would be at church in the morning it was arranged that if we were able to get over the following morning she would come round to Hannafore after the service, climb over the rocks at low tide and yell to us, who in turn would have clambered as far as possible to the low tide on our rocks, and yell back at her. The reason for this quite unnecessary assignation eludes me, especially as we should, if we did make the island on the morrow, be more than fully occupied heaving furniture frantically against time, as the tide came in, and we should have to catch it. One can only put it down to "island fever".

Our gentleman friend of the night before—he of the generator, heli-copter and pipelines-over-the-sea ideas—must also have been possessed of island fever for he too was round bright and early. In fact he was embel-lishing on his schemes when Wren arrived at 9 a.m. Wren, who himself was not short on ideas, his favourite being the building of a harbour wall to make landing in rough seas possible, listened goggle eyed as we all sipped coffee. The post brought us back to reality. Before the three of us, plus Toby, drove into Plymouth we learned that my camera, which I had at last sent off to my photographic suppliers, was probably a dead loss, and the estate agents had so far been unable to sell our house, and again wanted us to drop our price. The camera was insured so its loss was not the disas-ter it might have been. As for the house, our bank manager was still friendly, in fact *very* friendly, for Babs had received a letter asking if she would consider keeping her current account with him after she had moved from the district. "It was the first time," said Babs, "that any bank has vied for the privilege of handling my overdraft." At that time teachers' salaries were hardly large enough to set the banking world alight and she was usually slightly in the red. Spring was not far off and with it, we hoped, shoals of house hunters. In any case we were not in the mood to worry—we were off to the Barbican from which the *Mayflower* had set sail. Clode's was just a few yards from the steps where this event took place and a plaque commemorated the event.

The chandler's was a fascinating place. One climbed down steps to an underground store that dated back to Nelson's time, and it was a veritable Aladdin's cave of maritime treasure trove. Led by the colourful figure of Wren clad in his red shirt and tall sea boots we clambered over piles of chains, ropes and pulleys and threaded our way past storm lanterns and a ship's locker and ship's figurehead that looked as though they too had been there since Nelson's day. At last Wren selected some chain that was to his satisfaction. This was measured by the fathom and Wren had six fathoms cut off, but to our surprise it was sold by weight. Weighing it was a long and cumbersome operation. We were even more surprised to find that the cost was only £3, for the length of chain and its girth made it look as though it was all set to tow the *Queen Elizabeth* at least. While the weighing, rattling and clanking was going on Babs and I explored this subterranean hoard of treasure. To our delight we found a loud hailer of a bygone age, one that in our imagination could surely have voiced the commands of Sir Francis Drake, no less. Fashioned long before the days of plastic and electronics it appeared to be made of a kind of tough whale hide—or perhaps that of some strange sea monster, we thought fancifully. Over a yard in length it amplifies with a resonance unmatched by a modern powered one we have since acquired, and many times has summoned folk from the other side of the island, or sometimes attracted, when necessary, the attention of a passing boat. We thought it more than a bargain at 15/–.

By this time ropes, plugs, links and thimbles (these last having nothing remotely to do with needlework) had been added to our purchases, and by the time it was all loaded into our estate Mini there was just room for Toby to perch on top of the mountain of chain. The weight made steering difficult and we more or less floundered back to Looe, rather like manouvering a tank through bogland. We counted ourselves lucky to make our way over the hills without incident, or being arrested. Toby, a dyed-in-the-wool conservative, as most dogs are, had a habit of objecting to anything that to his mind was "different". "Different" embraced anyone from a parson in a dog collar, a kilted Scotsman, a sari-clad Indian lady, boy scouts and anyone coloured. They were all classed in his doggy world as definitely odd. He voiced their non-acceptability by barking loud and long from the back window of the car until the object of his derision had receded far into the distance. Unhesitatingly Toby now added a pile of chain to his list of offenders, especially as he was perched on top of it, and to show his displeasure he howled his head off all the way back to Looe. Added to our very real fears that we might swerve into a ditch were the worries that not only might we be arrested for drunken driving but that we should be reported to the R.S.P.C.A. for transporting a dog in chains along the Queen's highway.

Luckily we made Looe without incident by lunchtime. Wren then unexpectedly announced that we could make a short trip to the island to take any light hand baggage or parcels. We had been haunting Nancollas's store for days to see if our gardening equipment had arrived. This had now come and the removal men must have lifted everything in sight for besides piles of neatly stacked flower pots were boxes containing odd bits of raffia, broken flower pot pieces and near empty cartons of fertilisers and the like. Strings of onions now festooned the bookcases and, well to the fore, we were pleased to see boxes of our seed potatoes. These last seemed ideal to take for, with a bit of luck. we might have an opportunity to plant some. The trip would also be an opportunity to check on the daffodils. It was a constant worry to Mr and Mrs Whitehouse that the daffodils, which often started to bloom at Christmas, would be up and we should not be there to deal with them.

Armed therefore with boxes of seed potatoes, which inexplicably seemed to us the only useful things we could take by hand, we boarded the *Orlando* accompanied by Zena, her husband Peter, Charles and Duncan, trailing our ten-foot metal boat as a dinghy. Toby we left by the fire as there was no time to get Ethrelda as a Toby sitter and at his age we did not want to expose him to arduous sea journeys. After his ordeal by chain in the morning he was in any case quite thankful to rest his weary head.

Once out of the shelter of the harbour, wild seas met us and we literally bounded over the rollers which clawed at us from all sides as they broke over us in clouds of stinging spray. This time we made for the comparative shelter of the jetty beach on the eastern shore of the island. This was protected by an arm of rocks from the westerly gale which was roaring through the Island Roads—the strip of sea between the island and the mainland at Hannafore. Great seas were smashing on the main beach where he had made our previous landing and we were thankful when we at last made the lee of the island. It was tricky, nevertheless, to climb over the side of the *Orlando*, down into the bucking metal boat. Wren rowed me over to the jetty, a kind of small concrete platform built on a shelf of rocks below cliffs that slope down to the sea. The jetty was buttressed by stout upright timbers while behind, rough hewn steps wound their way to the top of the cliff where a path led to the jetty cottage and on to the Island House above and beyond. The posts were designed for tying up a boat—but on a calm day. Today the westerly gale backwashed the seas round the island and together with the ground swell from the spring tide the sea raced past the jetty like an express train. Very skilfully Wren managed to manoeuvre and juggle the metal boat into one of these runs. As we swept past the jetty on the crest of a breaking roller at breakneck speed he yelled "JUMP! Grab a post—it's slippery!" With the abandon of despair I flung myself onto the jetty clinging with both arms round the nearest post as the metal boat shot past from under me. I managed to haul myself on to the jetty which was indeed as slippery as black ice from algae built up over the winter months with rain, and the seas sweeping over it with spring tides. I managed to slither my way on to the steps to await for Babs to be decanted. Wren however had decided that it was too dangerous to land anyone else at the jetty.

I watched apprehensively as he rowed the metal boat with Babs on board between the rocks and over the breakers on to the jetty beach. Massive mounds of seaweed were being piled up on the beach by the crashing rollers. Babs, who was poised in the bows ready to land, now rolled over the side and let the surge of seaweed float her ashore. The others, plus the boxes of seed potatoes, were now landed on the beach too, but Wren, who had found the trip more hazardous than he had expected, would only allow us twenty minutes ashore.

Quickly we chitted out the potatoes, made a hurried tour of the nearest daffodil fields, none of which appeared to be in bloom, then prepared to launch ourselves back over the surging seaweed breakers. Following the custom of the Queen and Prince Philip, Babs and I elected to embark separately on the two trips necessary to transport us to the *Orlando* moored out beyond the rocks. One of us, we reasoned, should try to survive to take over the occupation of the island if ever the elements permitted that day to dawn. Once over the tricky business of negotiating the breakers crashing on the narrow rock channel and boarding the *Orlando*, heaving in the swell, the journey back to Looe harbour seemed comparatively calm and secure, although punctuated with sickening lurches to starboard and unexpected flights into mid air followed by crashes that half drowned us in sheets of spray.

As the sum result of this quite hazardous journey was the landing of a box or so of seed potatoes and a negative search for daffodils we did not feel particularly exultant as we trudged back to the cottage to change into dry clothes once more. We would have been even less elated if we had known that these potatoes, which we later planted with much care, would be stricken with a blight which that year swept the whole country. I doubt whether we harvested more than seven pounds that were edible. In time, labour, and expense no potatoes could surely have cost so much before or since. As at that time we rarely ate potatoes because we were on a diet I think if the phrase "Is your journey really necessary?" had not already been coined we should have invented it ourselves there and then.

Babs was up early the next morning, Sunday, in case Wren called for them to inspect the sea at Hannafore. This would be the last chance for a big move of stores before the next spring tides due in two weeks' time on 30th January. With Mr Nancollas on his tail we knew that Wren would have a try if it were at all possible, although we did not think that there was the remotest chance of yesterday's seas dying down for days even if the gales abated.

High tide at 5.24 a.m. passed and there was no sign of Wren. Lying in bed and listening to the 6.55 a.m. weather forecast I knew why. It forecast storms—gales everywhere—a wild day, becoming more severe. That was enough for me and thankfully I turned over and snuggled down into the pillow. It was as well Babs was up and dressed, for Duncan, his appetite whetted by yesterday's jaunt, called to say that he had walked over to Hannafore and it was quite calm there. This I could not believe. However, Babs and he went to see if perhaps Wren was on the *Orlando* getting it at the ready. As he was not they climbed high up the steep steps to Chapel Ground where his cottage was perched on the side of the Downs. Wren in fact was only just getting up as he too had heard the forecast, but taking Duncan at his word about the state of the sea at Hannafore he said he would be ready in half an hour. Never at my best in the morning I yelled through the ceiling from my warm and cosy bed that I was not going. Babs yelled back from below that she was not going to climb all the way up to "Bali-Hi", the name of Wren's cottage, to tell him so. A most inapposite name for the cottage in the circumstances, I muttered into the pillow.

Meantime Wren and Duncan both arrived for Babs to drive them round to Hannafore so that Wren could inspect the sea for himself. I now arose and dressed, not to get ready but to protest. After all, I wanted to live on the island, not be washed up there as a drowned corpse. A few minutes later they returned and Wren announced categorically that "No fisherman in Looe would go out in a sea like that." Coming from Wren that was a concession indeed; not that we had seen any other boats at sea since we had come at Christmas for the gales had scarcely abated from one spring tide to another. Nevertheless, as I had been the lily-livered one of the quartet I was relieved to hear on the 9 a.m. news, "A wild night everywhere. No one should be out, especially at sea." A comment that was tailor-made for me and confirmed my belief in telepathy.

As consolation Wren brought in the coils of rope purchased the day before and, doing deft things with spikes and thimbles, showed us how to splice rope. The outboard motors were brought out from behind the sofa and in no time at all the one downstair room of our "two up and one down cottage" began to resemble the deck of a ship. The usual stream of visitors now began to call. Zena followed by Charles, Ruth and her mother on their way to Mass, and Mr and Mrs Whitehouse relieved to know that the daffodils were not yet ready for harvesting but still anxious about how we were going to manage the generator without a man. After copious mugs of coffee followed by homemade wine Wren, Duncan, Charles, Ruth, Babs and I walked round to Hannafore at low tide to find the channel Mr Whitehouse had told us they used for rowing the daffodils across to the mainland when it was too rough to make the harbour.

It was easy to find the landmark he had given us on the mainland at low tide for it was in fact the sewerage channel. Fortunately it did not appear to be functioning, which was just as well since it was difficult to keep our feet on the slippery rocks and wet seaweed. We made out way beyond it and now had to find our way among a labyrinth of rocks, all the time keeping a bearing on a point of the island which was the landmark for that side. Unfortunately in mid-channel we were almost mown down by a storm of hailstones, and wet, cold, bruised and all but bleeding we slithered back over the seaweed festooned rocks and returned to the cottage to dry out. It would not have been everyone's idea of a Sunday morning walk and we felt that we had done enough pioneering for one day.

We were joined for lunch by Duncan, a lad of many talents and interests, one of which we had in common and appealed to me enormously—the making and flying of kites. The top of the island seemed an ideal place for kite flying and I only hoped that there would be time to indulge in this pastime. As this was one of the few interests not shared by Babs she rather thought not.

Wren had invited the three of us up to "Bali-Hi" for tea, and, while his wife provided the eats, Wren entertained us with further demonstrations of rope splicing and knot tying. I, for one, had never inherited Dad's aptitude in these skills. I had never been a girl guide and although I had mountaineered among the glaciers and ice peaks of the Alps where the correct tying of a knot was a matter of life and death, and although we had been given instruction during our training period in the W.R.N.S., the art of knot tying had always eluded me. Babs, without the benefit of life in the Navy or the experience of dangling over the edge of a crevasse or precipice on the end of a rope, made a far more apt pupil. Probably due to her penchant for needlework, by the end of the evening she had become quite adept. Nevertheless we had a most enjoyable time; our education had been considerably broadened, for Wren expounded in detail on other maritime matters, all of which we found instructive and fascinating, and it was, to say the least, a novel way of being entertained to Sunday afternoon tea.

Chapter 6
Alarms and excursions

Until the next spring tides were due we reckoned that islandwise it would be a period of marking time; tidying up in Nancollas's store and bracing ourselves for ordeals to come being the order of the day—a lull before the storm we were sanguine enough to hope. In the event there was no lull. Babs, of course, was busy at school finding her bearings and plotting her course there. Certainly a great deal of sorting went on in the store every day. I was round there every morning lugging out some essential that we needed and, ably helped by Zena, did a lot of re-stacking. This was necessitated by the fact that there was a hole in the roof of the store, through which the rain poured. It took a great deal of ingenuity to shield our more precious possessions under hardier ones and much expenditure of energy and sure footwork to achieve this without disaster to the furniture or ourselves.

It was predictable, too, that we should continue to have an increasing number of visitors to our cottage, offering their advice and expressing the usual fears on our behalf. We made sure that we had a good supply of coffee and plenty of homemade wine on tap; not that the hospitality was all one-sided for we received many invitations to visit our new friends.

What we had not anticipated was what can only be described as an adult version of the childhood "whispering" game. In this we recalled you sat in a circle: someone whispered a short sentence or phrase to the next child who in turn whispered what he or she thought had been said to the next one and so on until the last one to complete the circle called out the final version. I suppose all of us as children have had hysterics at what to one's simple childish mind seemed screamingly funny. We now had hysterics of a different kind as our succession of visitors passed on to us the versions they had heard of our supposed plans. Listening to these we felt it prudent to say as little as possible, make suitable disbelieving clicking noises with our tongues, pass the coffee and comment that our only plan was to move ourselves and our furniture over to the island as soon as possible, and that this seemed highly unlikely until the summertime—if then.

We were dumbfounded therefore when a complete stranger stopped us in the street and said that he had had pointed out to him exactly where we were having the airstrip laid down for the landing of aircraft. Next, Mr Sargent, the Harbourmaster, approached Babs and told her that we should have to consult him and get his permission, which he was highly unlikely to give, to build a harbour, as nothing must impede the fishing fleet when they took to sea.

Airstrips! Harbours! A landlocked fishing fleet—the mind boggled. And all because of a few pots that at that moment seemed to have no chance of being thrown at all except in the teeth of a gale in desperation. After all, with only a few months' potting behind me we hardly expected hordes of devotees to come on pilgrimage from all four corners of the earth to pay homage at the feet of my genius, and an airstrip *and* a harbour could be preparation for no less. Babs, of course, told Mr Sargent, a kindly and helpful gentleman, that he had been misinformed, that his fears were quite unfounded as we did not anticipate that our modest income of a teacher's salary and my pension would run to the building of a harbour in the foreseeable future.

Still reeling from these wild rumours of our supposed plans we suddenly found ourselves a subject-for discussion at the Harbour Commissioners' meeting. And we only knew about this when someone brandished a copy of a West Country Sunday paper at us. In this was a report of the meeting at which Mrs Couch, the president, said that she had been approached by Looe boatmen as they viewed with grave concern the danger to which their for-hire boats would be subjected if they were allowed to land on the rocky coast of the island. Mrs Couch herself expressed equal concern. The report did not give any further details of the discussion, but it was enough to fill us with indignation and wrath. The other rumours had us curled up with laughter as they were so ludicrous, but this was more serious; it was a report in print of an official item on the agenda of the Harbour Commissioners' meeting. This was a matter we knew we must do something about.

When I first read the account I could not wait for Babs to get home from school for I had only seen the Sunday paper on the Monday morning after our rope splicing demonstration. Meantime, to work off some of my indignation, Ruth and I went round to the quayside to make an attempt at getting one of the outboard motors started on the fibre glass dinghy. Ruth, unusually for a girl, loved engines and things mechanical, and soon succeeded. Spurred on by, her example I gingerly had a tug, but, remembering the account in the paper, pulled much more violently and the thing miraculously leapt into life. This for some inexplicable reason gave me the inspiration for what we should do—write a letter to the papers, of course! After all, wasn't this what every "Perplexed Blue-eyed", "Distraught Mother of Six", or "Indignant Ratepayer" did when they had a grievance to air or a problem to be solved? We certainly, as "Irate Islanders", qualified for the former, and for our money, the latter too. Accordingly I dashed back to the cottage and drafted a letter, with a copy and a covering letter to be sent to Mrs Couch, for courtesy's sake. After all, she could have done no less than report the grievance made to her and the boatmen had every right to lodge a complaint and express their concern if what they had heard was true. This was the rub. We had no intention of allowing boats to land on our island. Like the previous owners, we intended to guard our privacy jealously. At most we thought that we might let a few privileged private parties of people interested in crafts come to view the pottery, for, simmering at the back of our minds, was an idea—that we should do our bit to keep crafts alive; that in time we might accommodate a few retired craftsmen who would not only make crafts to sell to help support themselves and the island but teach their skills to others. These summer schools would, we hope, make the whole project economically viable. In addition these craftsmen would each contribute something to the common good according to his ability eg. till the land, keep goats, bees and poultry, or be responsible for carpentry, engines etc. All this might be possible with some chance of success if we aimed at a "floating community," we thought, whereby our craftsmen might come for a season only and longer if it worked well. We had no illusions about the difficulties of communal life and knew that its success hinged entirely on the character and personality of each individual and depended hardly at all on the trials, privations and disasters that might have to be endured.

Of one thing we were certain—the island must be kept inviolate—there must be no commercialism. Before the banners of Conservation, Ecology, and Environment were fluttered before the urban populace we were hoisting our own little flag and were determined that any income we might derive from our crafts would be used to help preserve the island as an unspoilt beauty spot. It was no wonder therefore that we were incensed that our modest and, according to our reckoning, worthwhile aims were misconstrued.

Babs on her return vetted the letter and added her comments. In essence it stated what our aims were, asked the press if they would refute these wild rumours that were circulating and suggested rather tartly that it would have been a good idea if someone had approached us about our supposed intentions before reports were officially made and broadcast based merely on hearsay. Furthermore if we did not get the backing of local bodies we would keep the island strictly private and allow no one to land at all, as indeed was and is our right as the owners of private property maintained solely by ourselves, without any financial assistance or grants, local, public or governmental—and a right furthermore that had been strictly preserved by previous owners. And why not? We have yet to meet anyone who would welcome any Tom, Dick or Harry to come and picnic in their back or front garden uninvited. Yet, as we were to find later, there are many who hold the oddest ideas about other peoples property—particularly if it consisted of an island.

Having written all this to our satisfaction we contacted Mrs Clemens, the local correspondent for *The Cornish Times*, a lady with whom we were acquainted. She came round like a shot and was indignant on our behalf. Not only would she re-write her own report intended for the weekly *Cornish Times* due out later in the week, based on our letter, but she would send a copy to the West country daily paper, *The Western Morning News*.

Suddenly it was as though we had set alight to a stick of gelignite. First *The Western Morning News* came out with banner headlines in the centre page "LOOE ISLAND—OWNERS MAKE STATEMENT." This was followed in other papers by similar reports and accounts. Everyone we met seemed to be waving copies of these papers excitedly at us. Later, private indignation meetings were held at odd street corners and outside shops— meetings to which we were invited to join—to protest because one paper had made no report at all. The anger quickly subsided however when this particular newspaper joined in and published our letter in full. This was only Tuesday but that same evening Westward Television flashed a picture of the island on the screen and quoted excerpts from our letter. This caused a great deal of excitement in Looe, for being mentioned on television was fame indeed, and we were the centre of many little group meetings in the baker's, the greengrocer's and the butcher's. At school the children were full of it and thrilled that their teacher had been quoted on T.V.

We, in fact, did not see the item for we had been invited that evening to Ruth's house to try some of her mother's home-made wine. We were also introduced to some friends, the husband of one of whom said that he gave us twelve months on the island and then we should give up—if we were not drowned beforehand! Although we were quite flattered, as we had heard that most of the fishermen only gave us three months, we replied succinctly that at the present rate of progress we doubted if we would even have taken up residence by then.

The next day we were asked if we would appear on Television that very evening. A car would call for us and take us to the studios in Plymouth. We politely declined, our main reason for refusing being that we should not have had time to have had our hair done—and this was not the last time we opted out of appearing on television for this reason. We were told what good publicity it would be, an incentive we have never appreciated for it sounded to us more like a commercial for a laxative or a breakfast cereal proclaiming how "good it was for you". Maybe it was all right for some, but we did not *want* publicity, and even if we had, the state of our hair was the over-riding factor.

Also, by return, we received a charming letter from Mrs Couch thanking us for sending her a copy of our letter to the press, wishing us well in our project and hoping that sometime she would be able to come over and visit us.

This particular furore died down as suddenly as it had arisen and was rather neatly finished off, we thought, by the receipt of a letter from the *Western Morning News* enclosing a postal order for 5/- for publication of our letter—the going rate at the time. How nice, we thought, to be paid for laying down the law. We made it, too, the first contribution to our Island Fund.

The furore did not so much die down as became superseded by another. Mr Nancollas called round to say that he had again arranged for a fisherman to take over the furniture and the expedition was all fixed up for the next day. We sympathised with him for we knew that he really needed his store for his auction sales, but we knew also that Wren would be needled to say the least. Either way we did not think that we should come out of the situation too well. If the furniture were taken out the next day would it—we dare not even ask—be left on the jetty or the beach, exposed to the elements? There would be no Wren to move it by the caterpillar tractor; Babs would be at school, as would be our schoolboy helpers, Charles and

Duncan. It seemed that either our furniture would be left high but not dry on the beach or Wren would feel impelled to have a go at the week-end whatever the weather. We knew that very little daunted him weatherwise; it was going to be a case of "Fasten your safety belts!" either way, for if the weather did foul up Wednesday it would surely worsen with the increasing spring tides due on Saturday.

Wren called in later and when we told him of the plan for tomorrow, as we expected, his generally cheery face blackened and he went off downcast and despondent. Later he returned his face beaming once more. "Good news," he announced, "Gales are forecast for tomorrow, and the wind is already getting up."

He was right, terrific snowstorms and floods hit the whole country that night. The next morning we found West Looe Quay under water and cars and boats were lined up alongside each other deep in the overflowing banks of the river just as they were on our first visit to Looe fourteen months ago. With the combination of gales, rain and winter spring tides the river could not contain the volume of water which was rising rapidly and fast approaching Nancollas's store. With some of our furniture wet from the leak in the roof above and now threatened with the overflowing river flooding in from below it did not seem to have much chance of surviving. Alfy Martin however assured us that all would be well for even if the water did reach the store they had storm barricades at the ready. What were we worrying about with only the ordeal by sea for our possessions to face? We were relieved now that the books were safely on the other side; but should we ever join them, we wondered wistfully, and would there ever be an opportunity to read them again?

The tension mounted as it always did prior to a proposed voyage over. Nevertheless there was nothing much we could do before Saturday so we were happy to accept an invitation to the home of Mrs Coon, the school secretary, to meet her husband who was a keen and knowledgeable amateur ornithologist. He had a rare collection of books, especially on his chosen subject, many first editions and beautifully leather bound priceless volumes which lined the wall of all the rooms and the hall. We had a splendid evening and looked forward to a visit from him to the island at a later date. This he subsequently made and we learned a great deal from him about the wild life of the island. It is sad to realise that we can learn no more from him.

We also paid another visit to Miss Kempster and Miss Hoyle who had invited us round for the evening. They were most interested in our project as Miss Hoyle herself did pottery and Miss Kempster, a retired headmistress, was having lessons in painting from a local artist. They have both been over to the island several times to see how we are progressing and never fail to buy a piece of pottery to help the Island Funds. Miss Hoyle, who came from a Looe family, actually had a relative who was one of those who was born in our No 1 cottage. We invited them round to tea the following week, an invitation which we gave with some misgivings for they had a very nice comfortable home perched a little way up one of the steep roads leading to the downs from the quayside, and it had a fine panoramic view of the river and harbour and the hills rising above East Looe. Our little home on the other hand, much as we loved it, currently resembled a cross between a railway station and the deck of a ship, a ship, moreover, halfway to shipwreck. The tiny cobbled courtyard, picturesque in less hectic days, could now best be described as a shunting yard; beyond our acquisitions which had overspilled there from the cottage there was no outlook at all except the side of a cottage looking down on us from its higher level—hardly, we thought, the setting for an "At Home".

On the way we made a diversion to the store to find a projector as Zena, who had by now introduced her brother George from East Looe to our little circle of "Islanders", wanted us to see some of his colour slides—close-ups of butterflies, birds and flowers. After much clambering about in the dark we found it but by the time we got back to the cottage it was too late for a film show, added to which certain parts of the projector and plugs were missing. The next morning I was despondently searching for these bits and pieces for it was cold and wet in the store when Ruth, knowing where to find me, arrived in great excitement as she had found a source of manure, an item for which I had sent out calls in readiness for our proposed mushroom growing. She knew someone who had a riding school and we could have as much as we wanted just for the fetching. Highly elated, we collected up some sacks of this rich by-product of the horse, then we carried it on to a clearing owned by her father, where there was much wood to be had for the picking-up. With great expertise she showed me how to split wood with a single blow and with the two choppers which she had thoughtfully brought along we soon had a good collection of firewood. Unfortunately it began to pour with rain and the wood got very wet. I had in mind to present some to Ethrelda who at her age felt the cold, and she enjoyed nothing better than to bask in the warmth of her open fire.

Even in Cornwall we were having flurries of snow in the rain, and the rest of the country was practically ice-bound. We called in at our cottage to dry the wood off by the fire and then, to finish our winter "harvest festival", we went by car to some nearby woods to gather some moss for Ruth's mother who wanted some for her flower baskets. Contrary to the saying about gathering moss I felt very much like a rolling stone. I had literally rolled from one minor activity to another as I waited for Babs to come home from school for the week-end so that we could prepare ourselves for the move that we anticipated Wren would call for the next morning, whatever the weather, which had shown no signs of improving.

It was fortunate that Zena postponed the film show, due to Peter having a cold, for Ethrelda called to ask if she and her daughter Muriel who was visiting her from "up country" could spend the evening with us. This of course did not prevent other visitors from popping in, including our friend of helicopter and pipe-lines-over-the-sea fame, Zena with her brother George who offered to bring private parties over in his boat the *Crilla*, and a couple of "up country" emigrants who had only just seen the reports in the press about us and thought we might be interested in reading them! Ruth also dropped in to pass on the message from Duncan's mother that if we should go to the island tomorrow we must on no account let Duncan use the caterpillar tractor as he was subject to epileptic fits. Finally Wren appeared to say, as we suspected, that he thought it might be possible to make an attempt in the morning. Mr Nancollas had been after him and as after this week-end the next spring tides would not be due until February 6th we knew, as a matter of pride, that Wren was after winning the "Nancollas Spring Handicap", fishermen aiming to pip him at the post or not. We managed to squeeze everyone into our tiny cottage and at one stage the room began to resemble an overloaded lifeboat, an illusion heightened by the howling wind and slashing wind outside and the talk of the proposed journey into the elements on the morrow.

Chapter 7

Storm noises—off stage and on

As high tide was not until 9.57 a.m. Wren called next morning at the reasonable hour of 8.30 a.m. and for the first time Babs took him round to
inspect the sea at Hannafore in almost broad daylight. Although a southerly gale was forecast Wren thought that we should be able to make it.
Since coming to live on the island we have come to dread a winter southerly gale perhaps more than any other for we are particularly exposed to
the south, and our bedroom and lounge are both facing in this direction. It
is a wind that always seems to blow at force 8, 9 or even 10; it rips off tiles,
blows down trees and is accompanied invariably by a slashing rain that
penetrates usually watertight windows, seeps through the roof and doors,
and generally makes life unusually unbearable. In a severe storm the sea
breaks over the cliff top, flinging seaweed and bits of rocks over on to the
end of the garden. The wind hurls itself against the window with such
violence that sleep is almost impossible, and when I have been alone on
the island it can be a daunting experience wondering what havoc the dawn
will reveal, or if one will survive till the dawn.

In my ignorance then I happily began to hum *Blow the Wind Southerly*. Now I can never hear that lovely song without thinking that Kathleen
Ferrier or the composer could never have experienced a southerly gale—
Cornish style. If I had the gift of composition I would certainly give it an
1812 tempi and ordain that none but a Wagnerian quartet should sing it
with organ accompaniment that would make the *Ride of the Valkyries* sound
like an afternoon jaunt in a pony and trap by comparison.

Knowing nothing of what awaited us we cheerfully went round to
Nancollas's store and helped by Charles, Duncan and Ruth began the task
of moving out everything that we thought we should want and Wren thought
he could manage, and put it on to the quayside. Now began the task of
lowering the furniture by ropes over the side and down into the *Orlando*. It
was as well Wren was so competent, as his crew consisted of we three
females and two schoolboys. Later we were joined by a passer-by, Den
Smith, who in the season ran a speed boat. While Wren lashed everything

down Babs and I went and did some shopping for food. We ran into Mr and Mrs Whitehouse who were still anxious on our behalf. In fact Mr Whitehouse offered to come over with us there and then to look at the machinery and show us how the generator worked. Knowing the state of his health and the fact that it was mid-winter we thought that this would be most unwise. Regretfully he had to agree, but we thought nevertheless how kind it was of them to take such an interest in our welfare. Of course they knew what difficulties we would be up against, and they found it hard to understand that in spite of their warnings and advice we should be insouciant about the whole affair. Knowing what we now know we would probably have been as concerned as they were. However, we would never have got to this stage or bought the island in the first place if we had weighed the pros and cons at every juncture. We had come from the wrong family to do otherwise or be put off by a few difficulties.

At last the *Orlando*, heavily laden with our precious possessions dangling precariously from furniture perched aloft the wheelhouse, nosed her way slowly towards the open sea. All went well at first although the sea was roughening as we left the shelter of the harbour. The furniture creaked ominously and there were the usual wild lurches as we crossed the bar. With each of these crashes Babs leaned over to hang on to a heavy antique chair that for some reason, probably an afterthought, was suspended over the stern and seemed in imminent danger of nose diving to the sea bed and becoming treasure trove for some deep sea diver of a future generation.

The troubles really began when Wren tried to beach the Orlando. This, . we have since realised, is never attempted by a sea-going boat of that size and with that draught on an open beach even in the summer on a dead calm day. As the island had no harbour a boat with the draught of the *Orlando* would moor off in deep water and landing would be made by dinghy. This of course was impossible with furniture to land. On the previous occasions Wren had skilfully beached the *Orlando* by bringing her in so far, moored off while she was still afloat and as the fast out going spring tide receded put down "legs" to keep the *Orlando* from keeling over as she was left high and dry. The difficulty now was that the sea was already making up fast with the outgoing tide, whereas one might have expected the southerly gale to break with the incoming tide in the late afternoon. The result was that great seas, made vicious by the ground swell, came running in slewing the *Orlando* round and in danger of bringing her broadside on. In the shallow water, as the rollers receded far out leaving her high and dry, helpless she might keel over. We only knew this with hindsight as we have many times had this difficulty with our own boat the *Islander* which is only a 22 ft motor boat, but as lethal as a torpedo as she charges helplessly with the speed of an express train in the raging surf that beats on these shores long after the gales themselves have abated.

All we knew at the time, luckily for our peace of mind—comparative peace of mind that is—was that we were in some difficulty. We had no real fears, for Wren, the most competent of seamen, would not engage in any situation unless he could forsee a way of dealing with it. But he loved a challenge and would accept any that would test his skill and ability. This proved to be one of many subsequent ones in which we were to be involved.

As we were hurled to the shore by the breakers Wren ordered Charles, Duncan and Ruth to leap over the surf on to the beach. As they floundered ashore Wren threw them a rope and roared to them to pull and hang on for dear life. Babs, and Zena who had joined us at the last minute, were ordered aft on to the deck head for balance, while I was detailed to take up my station amidships, for ballast presumably, ready to be sent scuttling wherever the need for weight was greatest. Wren himself disappeared astern.

Suddenly he yelled "It's my transom!" above the roar of the sea as the *Orlando* was swept out with the tide. For one moment I thought he was referring to a part of the male anatomy about which I had not heard and which was now at risk. Then it passed through my mind that perhaps it was a Cornish expression for trousers and that they were being ripped off by the breakers. Suddenly I realised from the gesticulating going on astern that it was a very important part of the boat that was in danger.

Meantime Charles, Duncan and Ruth with heels dug into the shingle were lying flat on their backs and tugging on the rope to try to keep the bows from slewing round. Wren roared at them at intervals, "PULL! PULL! HARDER" and as their heels scrunched even deeper into the shingle and they lay even flatter on their backs they looked for all the world like the losing team in a tug of war. Babs and Zena bobbed up and down on their precarious perch while I was slung around like a sack of potatoes as I clung to the deep freeze, of all things.

Wren at long last managed to steady the boat and by much heaving by the younger generation and skill on Wren's part, with a mighty scrunch the *Orlando* was at last beached with her legs down to keep her upright.

Wren seemed quite happy, so presumably the transom had been saved. This operation of beaching the *Orlando* had taken about an hour and by now the sea was far out. As soon as we had scrambled ashore I took photos, but we were distressed to find many dead gulls on the beach, victims of the furious wind—a sight unfortunately to which we have now become somewhat inured, so common is it during the long months of winter gales.

Wren soon had the caterpillar out and he, Charles and Duncan, unloaded and began the long haul of rumbling up the steep shingle path from sea level to our house on the cliff, possibly a third of a mile trailing loads of furniture. Ruth was left on the boat as "look out", though looking out for what it was difficult to conjecture. One thing was certain: it would not be for the fishing fleet or any other craft except possibly a fugitive Russian submarine for I was willing to swear that there was nothing afloat around the coasts of Britain that day except ocean going liners or ships of the Royal Navy making hard for port.

Zena now came into her own and took charge of the kitchen, for the simple reason that she was the only one slim enough to weave her way among the packing cases, washing machine, deep freeze, refrigerator, bookcases and other large pieces of furniture all of which were festooned with smaller articles. As the boys piled more and more furniture and boxes into the kitchen and then into the hall we were in danger of being incarcerated for the rest of our natural life. With the brilliance born of despair we now evolved a system of self preservation for the claustrophobic among us. Two of us managed to fight our way out and as the boys pushed more and more furniture through the open door Zena tossed articles and books over the increasing mountain of what is quaintly called artefacts to us. We then loaded these into wheelbarrows and trundled them down to what was once a barn and has now become our craft room. So we established our first transit camp on the island. As a brickmaking machine nestled alongside wine-making equipment, a telescope and a soil sterilizing stove we did have a passing thought about what archaeologists of the future would make of this little lot as with puzzled grunts they unearthed the remains in perhaps the year 4000.

This operation was going very well and Zena had just pioneered her way across the kitchen to the stove to make a nice cup of tea all round when two things happened simultaneously. Babs and I, who had cunningly wormed our way to the scullery sink by the back door turned on the tap to fill the kettle which Zena had more or less lobbed over to us. The water that gushed out was a foaming brown liquid with a most vile stench that had us retching on the spot. We looked at it, horrified, and Wren barked over his shoulder as he roared off in the caterpillar like a latter day charioteer, "Everyone to the boat at once! The gale has got up and the sea is rough!"

The rain lashed at us as we clambered on board. Darkness fell. Wren clad in oilskins and sou'wester had us all lined up, as with grim face he told us exactly what we were to do.

"It is not just a question of saving the boat," he announced, "it is a matter of life and death!" He explained that we could not take off until there was sufficient water to float the *Orlando*. Tremendous seas were running in, crashing over us from the west and threatening to capsize us. The next moment they sucked back leaving the *Orlando* high and dry and, without the support of the sea, she was again in danger of keeling over.

"Do what I tell you, instantly!" he ordered. At that moment a huge sea crashed down on us. "Everyone to port!" yelled Wren. We all hurled ourselves over to the other side of the boat. "To starboard!" roared Wren. And we all scrambled back again. We could not anticipate which way we had to throw ourselves for in that broiling sea the breakers came in all directions and Wren hung over the side judging to a nicety exactly where and when the next roller would break over us. We were not allowed to move except as ordered, for it would have upset the balance of the boat. We could see huge breakers creaming over the rocks even in the darkness—it was that wild. Rain poured down our necks in spite of sou'westers and oilskins, but we had much implicit faith in Wren that in the short intervals we sat as though we were in a bus and Zena and I had a long discussion about piles, of all things, inspired by the fact that we were sitting in pools of an icy mixture of rain and sea water. And so we went on hurling ourselves to port or starboard as directed. There was no confusion as to which was which for we knew it was the opposite side to where we happened to be; we just pitched ourselves bodily across from one side of the boat to the other and hoped for the best. It was fortunate that Wren did not spice his orders with "Abaft! Abeam! Hard Astern! Amidships!" or whatever, for we surely would have finished up doing a nautical version of the Lancers or the Grand Old Duke of York.

Wren did clever things with his precious transom and at last, after about an hour, and with much creaking and lurching of the gallant *Orlando* we could feel deep water under us and we were afloat! Once away from the shelter of the western rocks of the island the full force of the gale hit us. Wren however looked happy and relaxed now that he had only the straightforward problem of a raging storm to cope with. In spite of a very rough passage indeed, when we were tossed about like discarded clothing, and sodden clothing at that, we finally sailed safely into Looe Harbour.

Wren, who is practically a teetotaler, came into *The Jolly Sailor* near the cottage and we all had a rum to warm us up. Wren now asked if Babs and I would come along with him to see his father to placate him, as Wren said that he would be very angry that he had been at sea on a night like this. Babs and I accordingly went along as a kind of buffer but we really could not think of anything to say that would make the expedition sound like a Saturday night pleasure trip. Mr Toms, for whom Wren had a great respect and affection, was very angry indeed. "You take risks," he said wagging his finger at Wren, "and one day you will meet an unlucky sea. No one else would think of going out in that weather. You should listen to what the old fishermen say before going out in a sea like that." We knew that it was a bit of bad luck that the southerly gale had blown up earlier than anticipated and we knew that Wren had dealt with the problems with consummate skill. To him it had merely been a challenge to his ability to cope with the situation. We did not think our opinion would carry much weight as we were the wrong sex, age and occupation to vaunt expert knowledge. So far we had not said anything helpful and in fact, apart from "Good evening", all I did venture to remark was that if Sir Francis Drake had listened to the old fishermen he would probably have finished by being just an old fisherman. Just then Wren's wife came in, presumably to see if her husband were still alive. The conversation then petered out and we all went home.

The next morning Wren turned up bright as a button to say he thought it was calm enough to make another trip. Luckily it began to pour with rain and as Wren does not like getting wet from plain ordinary rain, he called it off. It was just as well for the sake of our remaining furniture, for at least by remaining in Nancollas's store only some of it would get wet.

We might justifiably have looked forward to a Sunday day of rest after the tribulations and labours of the day before, but it was not to be. From the word go the usual constant stream of people began to call, headed by the Whitehouses, who said that the whole of Looe was talking about our exploit. Most of the day we politely handed round cups of coffee as we listened to everyone's opinion, the consensus of which appeared to be that we were quite mad, that we were hardly likely to survive long enough to take up residence on the island, and that if we did, it was reiterated that after three months we would have "had it". It appeared that half the population had been watching from Hannafore the voyage of *The African Queen*, as the indomitable *Orlando* had been universally dubbed. No one had apparently expected us to return alive. Before the coffee finally ran out Wren brought in a little light relief by hospitably inviting Babs and me on board the *Orlando*, as he had stripped down the engine and he thought we might like to see it. "Soho, here we come!" we exclaimed gaily as we poured the last dregs of coffee down the sink and made tracks for the quayside for the "stripping". "Your transom's very 'andsome," I volunteered, bringing in rather aptly, I thought, the Cornish expression to describe anything praiseworthy. Then I left Babs, as the more mechanical one, to appreciate the finer points of the intestines of the hospitalized and surely weary *Orlando*.

Chapter 8

Social and unsocial interludes

The next day we met Mr Nancollas who was a bit irate because not every-thing had been removed from his store. When we explained what a tricky operation it had been to move even one load he instantly mellowed and invited us into *The Jolly Sailor* for drinks. He had a lot of worries on his mind for, as Chairman of the Council, he was responsible for arranging a memorial service for Winston Churchill on the following Saturday. Nev-ertheless he said that he was arranging a cocktail party for us and Friday February 5th was fixed as a hopeful date for our farewell launching party.

As it was a bright sunny day, although bitterly cold with the rest of the country still under snow and ice, Ruth and I thought that we would try out the outboard motor on the fibre glass dinghy again and if it were calm enough go out to the island in it. I had been out to the island before in a small boat when a friend came to visit us in October. Babs and I had navi-gated keeping to the same channel between what we thought were beds of seaweed as the professional boatman had taken us. It was as well that our judgement had proved correct for what we thought was seaweed darken-ing the sea round the beach were in fact reefs of rock and the channel through them very narrow indeed. What we did not know until we came to live on the island was that winter gales can change the whole outline of the foreshore many times, covering some rocks with shoals of sand and sea-weed and exposing others that had not been seen for many years. Chan-nels and landing points have to be carefully assessed and can be quite different between one summer and another, depending on the ravages of the winter seas. Knowing none of this at that time I was quite optimistic at steering through the "sea-weed beds" again if the seas of the week-end had died down enough for us to get out of the harbour.

I like rowing and feel at home in a boat, but I am only used to the conventional wooden row boat. I was therefore disconcerted to find that a fibre glass boat bounces on top of the water like a cork and reacts to the slightest movement of its occupants. As Ruth and I took it in turns to pull at the starting cord of the outboard motor, with both our weights and that of the motor in the stern, the bows pointed skywards and with each unsuccessful tug it felt that we might go spiralling upwards into outer space at any moment. When in addition the boat started to leak I decided that perhaps it would be unwise to make an island trip. With the help of Zena who had appeared as though conjured up like a spirit from the deep I stepped out on the quayside. Ruth decided to have another go at getting the engine started. This she successfully did, but for some fathomless reason, as the boat got under way it meandered slowly in semi-circles, finally fouling the ropes of the *Orlando*. We managed to get it disentangled, I pulling from the quay. Ruth disembarked, and we decided to call it quits for that day. All this time we were watched by some of the fishermen on the quayside. Not one of them made any remark but I did wonder what they thought of our antics, especially when I listened to the weather reports and heard that wild seas were still lashing our coasts, and in particular in the Southwest.

Zena and I had arranged to go to the Catering Exhibition at Truro on the following day, with a view to laying up stores in bulk. The island seemed so inaccessible that we were now planning to take up residence there as though we were going to the Antarctic with no hope of seeing "dry land" again for a year at least.

It therefore was not strictly necessary to have a demonstration of an ice cream making machine, but we were fascinated by being able to get cornets out of it fully charged with ice cream. Regretfully we decided that it would not fit in with our plans—varied though they were. Also, it cost £8000.

Next our attention was caught by the Hammond Organ display. This seemed a "must" for the future. We tried one out that took our fancy and as the chords swelled and echoed round the Exhibition we got quite carried away until we found that it cost £1000. The salesman then introduced us to one that only cost £600, but that one did not appeal to us half as much. I then explained that what with an overdraft, a bridging loan and mortgages I for one could not afford one at all. The salesman did not mind a bit and offered to bring one over to the island to demonstrate. He said that it did not matter how long we left the idea in abeyance for he found that if people were really interested, as we obviously were, they would buy one eventually although it might be after an interval of years. Up to a point he was right. A few years later Zena did *buy* one and many times Babs from the cottage has heard the mellow notes of hymns wafting across from Zena's house on the other side of the Square. The salesman, if he should read these words, must forgive me, for although I, too, eventually bought an organ, it was (alas! for his sales), a church organ, the acquisition of which and its removal to the island almost deserves a chapter to itself when the time comes to relate it.

So far we had only looked at equipment that depended on electricity. As no one thought us capable of running the generator anyway perhaps it was just as well that we transferred our attention to food. The weather was still bitterly cold and we had negotiated icy roads to get to the Exhibition, so bulk soup figured largely in our purchases. In fact the consignment we bought that day lasted us for five years on the island and remained in good condition to the end, and a gargantuan tin of salt was only finished last year. I acquired a lot of free samples, made some good contacts and, as the Exhibition was open for the rest of the week, I told the various salesmen and demonstrators that I should be back with my sister if we did not manage to make a trip to the island.

The next day I spent quite a time in Nancollas's store looking for various articles. We had now been in the cottage since before Christmas and there was always something we were needing for our enforced stay on the mainland. On one visit I took the young assistant from the television shop as somewhere in the store were two television sets; one, which had been given us, needed overhauling and putting in working order, and our own, which was now required for Saturday. This was the day of Winston Churchill's funeral and Ethrelda had asked if she could come and watch it on television. Luckily neither set appeared to have suffered from the leaking roof, for they had been well protected by the removal men in the first place.

Wren called on Friday to say that the wind was in the East, a direction hated by all the local boatmen. In any case, he said he did not intend to try for a move the next day; he did not think that it was quite the thing to have an expedition over to the island on the day of Churchill's funeral, so he was going to move furniture for his father instead. His reasoning being, we supposed, that moving his father's furniture was a humdrum, run of the mill chore, whereas a move over to the island could be rated as an epic Saturday spectacular providing entertainment on a grand scale for the gallery of locals at Hannafore.

So on Saturday morning Babs and I prepared to make another visit to the Catering Exhibition, but we were not surprised that Ruth and her mother, whom we had invited to accompany us, did not turn up, for the roads were icier than ever and their house at Sunrising, on the hills above Looe, would be virtually icebound. We were late starting. For one thing we were held up by the usual round of visitors offering advice, help and the customary hair tearing about how we were going to manage on the island. We suspected that in some cases it was a matter of finding out if we were still alive and if so whether we had been carted off to the looney bin. After that it was difficult to get the car started and when Babs finally got it going Ruth turned up on foot and was most surprised to find that although we had not gone, we were still going! It was too late for her to negotiate the mile climb up to Sunrising and slide down again with her mother, so Babs and I set off, skating carefully round the bending 40 mile run into Truro.

We need not have bothered about being late because out of respect for Churchill the Exhibition was not opening until 2 p.m. Babs was most impressed with the Exhibition. She approved the mammoth orders, whisked me firmly past the Hammond Organ Section, and did the round of the free samples. Most of the demonstrators remembered me and were pleased to meet Babs, for the fact that you are going to live on your own island acts like a magic password. It puts one in a different class from those who merely own a Rolls Royce, a swimming pool and a villa in the South of France or the Costa What-have-you, judging by the effect it has on people. If only they knew that financially it was, in our case, done by mirrors, and living on it a cross between *The Birth of a Nation*, and *Sunday Night at the Palladium* with overtones of *Alice in Wonderland*.

Our favourite stand that bitter cold afternoon was the Cornish Mead display, the samples there not only warming up our chilled blood but inspiring us to set ourselves up with a few bottles to take back with us as an insurance against the cold.

Ethrelda asked if she could bring her daughter, Muriel, to watch the recording of the funeral that evening. We put out some refreshment plus some Cornish mead and, having installed our visitors, went over to Zena's for the postponed showing of the slides. It may seem odd to leave guests to entertain themselves, being absent hostesses so to speak, but the truth was that we did not want to watch the funeral. I think we felt that it might bring home to us what the outcome of our own little flirtation with destiny might be. Zena, who had been with us on some of our more hazardous expeditions possibly felt the same for she did not intend to watch it either— hence the film show of birds and flowers—not, we thought, a disrespectful

119

entertainment. Around 10.30 p.m. her brother George and his wife, having shown us some very fine slides, now expected to see the late showing of the day's solemn proceedings so we excused ourselves on account of our neglected guests. On the way over we ran into Wren who, with his wife, was trundling some of his father's furniture in a truck, so even that little chore had been relegated to the hours of darkness, when the day of national mourning was finally over.

As Wren had forecast, an easterly gale blew up on the Sunday so we now had just one more week to wait for what we hoped would be the penultimate move with furniture before we took up residence and prove at first hand how we would make out on *Desert Island Discs*, a programme that never failed to fascinate us. We were keyed up with excitement, and as far as we could see the intervening week would be a social one culminating with the cocktail party on Friday.

First Miss Hoyle and Miss Kempster were coming to tea on Monday, February 1st. The date made us realise what a very-long month January had been and how much had happened since leaving Surrey just before Christmas even though we were still living on the mainland. Now, although it will have been apparent that during this time we had been involved almost non-stop in entertaining—that is, when we were not actually on the high seas or marooned on the gale lashed shores of our island—these were the first guests we had actually *invited*. Therefore we felt we must put on some sort of show. By this we did not mean that we should bring out the best linen and china that in any case was still in Nancollas's store, but we did want them to feel that they were not only welcome but expected. It was all very well to scream at droppers-in, "MIND THAT ROPE!" while you handed round coffee in mugs rinsed out under the tap and offer biscuits, if any, from a packet. Our regulars had not only come to expect this reception, but actually liked it, for it made them feel at home. If on the other hand you are an invited guest you do at least expect a chair to sit on, and not have a pile of debris tipped off on to the floor before you can do so. Ruth therefore volunteered to come and help do some housework before our guests arrived. Neither of us claimed housework as our forte, having other interests to occupy our time, but we set to with a will. We swept out the sand and seaweed, made sure the rope was stowed well away, made neat piles of Ethrelda's sticks of wood drying by the fire, and after a thorough do of dusting and polishing, the room would certainly have passed muster for a new "daily" if she was coming for the first time to clean up. The only problem was what to do with the sacks of manure. If we put it out in the courtyard it would spoil the picturesque look for, bearing in mind that Miss Hoyle's aunt had been born in our cottage next door and she might have looked on the visit partly as a sentimental journey into the past, we had stuffed everything that was in the courtyard out of sight or carted it round to Nancollas's store. So for once the courtyard did not look like a transit camp and was as picturesque and charming as the day we had first seen it framing the top half of the vendor of the cottage in the horse box door. We sniffed at the bags. There was no smell so we shoved them behind the sofa with the outboard motors and coils of rope.

Ruth had just rapidly and discreetly disappeared out of the courtyard when our guests arrived, accompanied by Babs who, just arrived from school, wore not only civilised clothes but a look of relief to find the usual shipwreck transformed into an old world fishermen's cottage again.

We had a very pleasant time and thoroughly enjoyed discussing among other things the local flora and fauna, for both our visitors were keen naturalists. Miss Hoyle lent us a book on lichen and fungi and will not have realised until she reads these words how close she was sitting to a relative of the real thing.

After they had gone Zena dropped in with some haemmorrhoid cream done up in Christmas paper in a Bisto tin, in case the need should arise, she said, after our mid-winter night ride sitting in pools of icy water! She almost did not come in for she thought she had come to the wrong cottage— it looked so tidy and respectable.

The next day should have been uneventful. We had been invited to spend the evening with Ethrelda and as there had been no drama on the high seas at the week-end, no frantic callers were expected forecasting doom and disaster. Having just acquired a book on *Cooking in Norway and Denmark* I had experimented with some quite ambitious open sandwiches, made some ice-cream with Saturday's free samples topped with banana, walnuts and cream, put it in the fridge and settled down to some wood carving with a piece of driftwood I had picked up on the island. It was an exciting shape. I decided it should be called Sun God of the Incas and had just inserted the edge of the chisel when something, I do not know what, made me look up. There in the doorway which had opened silently stood the figure of a man. Something seemed to clutch at my heart. Nevertheless I said "Good morning," but there was no answer. An eerie feeling crept over me as the man neither moved nor spoke. I put down my Sun God of the Incas and stood up. The thought flashed through my mind that perhaps as my blade incised into the wood I had conjured up a spirit from the ancient world, an angry god who objected to my tampering with their sacred relics of which this might well be one. But the figure in the doorway did not emanate sunrays nor belch forth wrathful clouds of smoke from its nostrils. It wore a raincoat, trilby hat and glasses. The face began to twitch and I gripped my carving tool just in case . . . Suddenly the man began to giggle, threw off his hat and glasses, spat out his orange peel teeth to reveal no sinister stranger—but Zena. After that we went over to her place to make some Cornish pasties and simmer down from laughter and hysterics which can be quite as exhausting as drama on the high seas.

Ethrelda was thrilled with her supply of firewood and we had a very pleasant evening by her fire as she told us tales in her rich Cornish dialect. In the middle of this a friend of hers called. She wore a red hat, a kind of tammy, and although she took her coat off and settled down she did not take the hat off. After she had gone Ethrelda volunteered the information that she never did take it off and the saying went that she kept all her money under it. I have often thought since that the same could be said about me because when the easterlies blow I have to practically live in a fisherman's woolly cap; the only difference being that mine would be stuffed with I.O.U.'s and final demands. Actually she had some nerve trouble for which later she had to go for hospital treatment. She was a very cultured lady, of good family and she had a beautiful speaking voice. It was fascinating to listen to her telling local folklore and especially so when she told us exactly where buried treasure was reputed to be on the island. Many times we had heard from local people about the buried treasure that they vowed was on the island. It was also said that there were tunnels leading to the mainland used by the smugglers in olden times. If all the tunnels that we had heard about existed the harbour master would be a sorely troubled man, for the sea would surely have drained away into this labyrinth of subterranean tunnels and the fishing fleet would be landlocked indeed and never able to put to sea again. One such was supposed to come out in the "Smugglers" restaurant in East Looe and only last year we were told that the owner had excavated it as far as the Banjo Pier. We could not wait to get on the island and look for the buried treasure and the tunnels ourselves, although often it seemed that that day would never come and I would spend the rest of my life in Nancollas's store and Babs would spend hers shuttling to and fro to Hannafore with Wren to inspect the state of the sea.

I had to make yet another visit to the store to hunt for evening shoes for the cocktail party, although I had doubts as to whether I would be able to get into them again after spending so much of my time in sea boots. Fortunately they did fit but it did seem strange to wear a cocktail dress again after practically living in jeans, a seaman's jersey, oilskins and a sou'wester.

We had an excellent evening. The guests chosen to meet us appeared to be bankers, hoteliers and financiers—people whom Mr Nancollas had thoughtfully decided might well be of assistance to us in the future.

In our former existence cocktail parties were a part of everyday life. One was inured and sipped drinks amid the rising murmur of small talk with no more effect than downing lemonade. As the drinks diminished and the noise correspondingly increased one would be stimulated into thinking that the inconsequential remarks tossed around were the quintessence of wit good enough for the West End stage. It was all, as these affairs are, rather frothy and transient and already half forgotten by the next day. Such light sophistication however was a thing of the past and I for one was out of training. At the end of the evening I suddenly felt very tired. I put it down to all the exertions of the past few weeks, the sea journeys, humping of furniture and all the acrobatics performed in Nancollas's store; it had finally caught up on me I told myself sleepily but happily. Whatever the reason, when we left all I wanted to do was to go home and fall into bed. This was not possible for we had been invited to go on to visit Mr and Mrs Bassett. Mrs Bassett was a colleague of Babs, and her husband, a geologist, was going to show us some of his collection of rocks and minerals. Naturally Babs was very keen as this expert knowledge would help her enormously with her stone cutting and polishing. We had not been there very long when suddenly right bang in the middle of a conversation I fell asleep. I was out like a light.

Waking suddenly I saw an array of sparkling chips of rock swimming before my eyes. "Ha!" I exclaimed, fishing out some dim memory of the long ago schooldays "Iron pyrites!" Incredibly they *were* iron pyrites and the remark might have saved the day but for the fact that I promptly fell asleep again. Mrs Bassett has been over to the island several times since and it may be just imagination on my part but it seems to me that she looks very thoughtfully at me when I reach for the homemade wine bottle to pour some out for my guests.

Chapter 9

Unrehearsed incidents

The next day when we hoped to move most of the remaining furniture the wind was in the north east and fresh, but although it was only the 6th of February the bitterness had gone out of the wind. It was not exactly warm, but the wind did not cut you in two.

We cleared Nancollas's store of everything but a motley collection of garden tools, some wine carboys and *the* bookcase, which Wren unfortunately thought might be too big for him to manage. The *Orlando* as usual looked overloaded and deep in the water as she moved down the river. Once out of the harbour the wind began to freshen, and going over the bar was tricky, the short high cross waves making us pitch, toss and bump. The furniture slithered to and fro across the open deck and once again we were drenched with sheets of spray. Surprisingly, when once we had crossed the bar we only took about ten minutes. The sea was relatively calm and the landing on the main beach was unbelievably without incident of any kind.

Once ashore we tried to get as much done as possible in the time. First we attempted to sort out some of the chaos of our previous visits, for on these occasions no sooner had the furniture and chattels been dumped at the house than there had been a dramatic cry from Wren of, "To the boat, there is a storm breaking!" The resulting pile-up was indescribable. It was now almost impossible to get in the front door and penetrate the jungle of bookcases, tea chests, wine jars and photographic equipment festooned with an incongruous mixture of smaller articles. So we made the decision that there was no alternative but to manhandle everything twice, if we ever hoped to sort ourselves out when at last we finally moved in. We therefore designated the ex-barn—the enormous room that led down some steps and along a passage to the jetty cottage—as a transit camp, the idea being that if we moved everything down there except furniture we knew we should need in the house, we could sort out our possessions at leisure when once we had taken up residence—not knowing, in our innocence, that leisure was the one commodity that would be forever in short supply.

While Wren, Charles and Duncan brought up the fresh intake from the beach Babs tried to organise a system to save space now and time in the future, and was dubbed Queen Bee of "Operation Wheelbarrow", while Ruth and I raced trying to sow seed potatoes. We had been told that the climate on the island is one month in advance of the Cornish mainland, which of course is well ahead of the rest of the country and traditionally the first island potatoes are sown on Boxing Day. It seemed imperative that we should try and keep as near to this tradition as possible, especially as Paul Shelley, the greengrocer, had said that he would give us 3/6d a pound for early new potatoes, a very high price indeed in 1965, and this of course was the wholesale price. The first suitable field we dug was full of last year's unlifted main crop and we tore off down the path to find somewhere else. We did this at the double expecting to hear the clarion call "To the boats!" from Wren at any moment. In doing this I fell over some disused machinery and equipment that spewed across the path in front of us. My foot caught in the handle of an old watering can and at the speed I was going I pitched headlong among the rest of the rusty debris, twisting my knee.

Falls are one of the everyday hazards of island life. Rough tracks and pitted shingle paths are the more luxurious ways of getting from one part of the island to another. More usually one has to slither over seaweed, rocks and shingle paths slippery with algae, or hack a way through undergrowth snared with bramble shoots like wire traps, or trip over hidden lumps of metal or tools carelessly cast aside by someone, not realising that grass can grow four or five feet high and entangle anything in its path. Track clearing and keeping the main paths negotiable is a perennial and never ending task, for in a climate where frost is virtually unknown nature unchecked is very bountiful, especially to her favourite subjects the weed family. Leave the weeding of a shingle path for but one season and it is back to rough grass by the following year.

The long-sighted brigade are at particular risk for they are always focusing well ahead. Perhaps that is why some of us are naturally conditioned to have eyes only for the distant goal and do not see the more immediate obstacles, and not necessarily in a purely physical sense. Whatever the reason, my knee was hurt and painful but not enough to stop us planting the potatoes which we did at breakneck speed. I even had time to stay behind and sow some broad beans and, hopefully, lettuce and chives.

As there was no dramatic call from Wren we managed between us to get quite a lot done that day and we also had a foretaste of the delights the island had to offer, for we sailed back to Looe on a warm, starry night that was just like summer. It was incredible for early February, especially as the rest of the country was still icy and in some cases snowbound.

It was so enjoyable that we asked everyone to come on a picnic the next day and decided that it was warm and calm enough to take Toby. There were only a few bits and pieces to transport and to my great joy Wren said that he would have a shot at getting the bookcase over. Zena and Peter were not free to come but Ruth's mother and father did, armed with seeds and plants and ready to give their expert advice, also Wren's wife Valerie and, of course, Duncan.

With some trepidation on my part we saw the bookcase lowered over the quayside with ropes on to the deck of the *Orlando*. Once on board it was roped and buttressed with various sacks of fertilisers and the ubiquitous bags of manure. It was the easiest journey we had had so far; nevertheless I had some bad moments when the bookcase slithered from one side of the deck to the other when we crossed the bar, in spite of being securely roped, and at one stage it looked in danger of tipping over the side. However it survived the journey safely and once on the island we went our different ways. I, for one, not having the courage to watch Wren disembark with the bookcase and engage in the delicate operation of hoisting it on to the trailer of the caterpillar and tow it up the steep and bumpy path to the house, left the beach and with some of the others went about our various activities. Ruth and her father explored the caves, and then he and Ruth's mother did a tour sizing up the planting possibilities. It was arranged that they would get sacks of peat with their next order and a supply of wooden slats for making up our own seed boxes. Some of last year's tomatoes in the unheated greenhouse were still ripening and we were looking forward to doing some cultivation in the exceptionally mild conditions that the island obviously enjoyed.

Wren spent some considerable time putting a new head on the tractor and having warned Duncan again not to attempt to use it, he managed to ease the bookcase into the "transit camp". There it stands to this day and very impressive it looks too for now it is a fine room. The one-time barn, which had also been a music room in which Myra Hess practised on the grand piano when she was a guest of a professor of music from the Royal Academy who then owned the island, had, when we came, seen better days. Some of the floorboards were rotten from the earth beneath and some of hardboard with which the walls had been panelled were growing a white fungus from the same reason. For many months it remained our transit camp. Now we have had the rotted hardboard replaced with pyrana pine panelling. It is a carpeted room and with the walls hung with original paintings, handwoven panels and antique swords, together with pottery gifts from craftsmen displayed on wooden or hessian-covered benches and tables and the room furnished with some antiques, a Regency chaise lounge, and dominated at one end by the bookcase, the general effect has a certain richness of style. On the cliff top of an island it is quite unexpected. Most visitors, having tramped up the shingle path from the beach, express delighted surprise when they enter and many are known to sit for their entire visit in the sunshine streaming through the big bay window, instead of exploring the island they have come to see. One local friend, Gwen Miles who visited us for the first time was amazed. "I expected a hut with sawdust on the floor," she said. One corner of which we are particularly proud is where Babs has a fine display of semiprecious stones which she has cut and polished and fashioned into jewellery for, buried treasure or no, the island is rich in natural treasure. To our great joy we have found, as we understand Myra Hess had before us, a wealth of semiprecious stones on the beaches, especially after the winter gales. Among these are topaz, cornelians, banded agate, rose and amethyst quartz. This is pulling aside the curtain for a peep into the future for on that day the room was completely bare but for an old kitchen sink lying carelessly in the middle of the floor and soon to be surrounded by a mass of our diverse possessions.

While the major operation of moving the bookcase in was going on I was busy in the greenhouse trying feverishly to sow as many seeds as possible. Consequently I was the only one near the house when I heard a terrific crash. I rushed round to the side of the house and found the caterpillar tractor lying on its side belching forth smoke where it had fallen from a high grassy bank, standing on which was a very shaken Duncan. He had not, it transpired, been able to resist the temptation to try out the tractor; it had veered off from the track and out of control had crashed over the high bank on to the path outside the kitchen window. Luckily Duncan had the wit to leap off in time and was unhurt. I was afraid that the engine might burst into flames or explode and set the house on fire and I got Wren on to the scene as quickly as possible. He at once turned the engine off and sent Duncan off for planks of wood. Wren then not for the last time showed his great skill at leverage. Just by the use of planks which we placed according to his instructions he was able to get the tractor upright again although it is so heavy that it cannot by brute strength be pushed even one inch. It was damaged of course and spare parts had to be bought and a great deal of Wren's time spent on it before it could be put to use again. In fact for many years it was never quite the same again and was liable to give up the ghost and stop dead in the middle of an important operation, Wren's fear was that this might happen on the beach below high water level and be impossible to move. It is only recently that Wren was able to bring someone over who was an expert on this type of machinery and was able to put it in first class working order, much to Wren's satisfaction, and it is now able to move two tons of solid fuel without the fear that it may all be swallowed up by the ever hungry sea. It must have been a major operation involving cranes and many men to deliver the tractor to the island in the first place, although presumably it would have been in working order and could be driven straight up the beach.

Some weeks after this incident Wren, wishing to try out his running repairs, in his usual confidence-inspiring way, actually got me driving the thing from the beach up the steep path with a ten foot sheer drop just a hairsbreadth away. There were these two things like joysticks; in one direction they acted as brakes, but propelled in another they actually steered the thing. With Wren standing on one foot on a bit of its anatomy somewhere behind me yelling directions in my ear in an inferno of noise that by comparison would make Concorde sound like a bumble bee, I drove it up the path and in a masochistic kind of way actually enjoyed it. No doubt this was partly due to the fact that I had *survived*. It did bring home to me vicariously why it is that most men are so engine mad, because the feeling of power it gives them.

That day Wren was very angry that Duncan had disobeyed orders but said very little, for Duncan was a nice lad—just a bit too enthusiastic. It certainly put us back a bit financially and it was a nuisance that we could never rely on the "crawler" as it was frequently called, for it was much needed for the transport of the all important diesel oil for the generator, but at the time we were only relieved that Duncan himself was uninjured for it might well have been an accident with fatal results. Duncan was only fourteen at the time and a boy keen for adventure. He helped us many times at weekends during his schooldays with great and unfailing enthusiasm. After he left school he had a full-time job and we saw little of him. A year or so ago as a young married man of twenty-one, still keen on the active life, he used to go skin diving and one day just outside Looe harbour he was tragically found drowned.

We sailed back to Looe that night in pitch dark and apart from the difficulty of climbing from the bounding metal boat on to the *Orlando* there were no difficulties of any kind. Toby had thoroughly enjoyed his day and even leapt from one boat to the other quite happily which, as his maritime experiences had been strictly limited to trips up the Thames (a mode of transport not readily acceptable to his doggy conservatism), was surprising. He obviously intended to be an islander and as such was prepared to accept the hazards this entailed.

Chapter 10
More stage props assembled for opening night

There was now just one more week to "D" day, for as the removal of our possessions was more or less complete we could see no reason why we should not take up residence. Wren, cautious for once, counselled us to stay overnight only on the Saturday, presumably so that we could find our bearings. Babs of course would have to return to the mainland for school on the Monday.

Meantime a busy week lay ahead of us. Zena and I plus Toby went into Plymouth on Monday to buy up-more provisions. First we went into Dingle's, a big store, and took Toby with us. Now Zena did not have a dog and was inclined to think that we made rather a lot of Toby; perhaps she was of the opinion, although she was too diplomatic to voice it, that we over-rated his intelligence. Whenever we left him in the car well blanketed from the cold, for he was, after all, thirteen and a half and with a heart condition, she would make such remarks as "Have you left him a book to read?" or "Look! he is waving goodbye to us." Toby decided that he had had enough of this sarcasm and intended to pull a few tricks out of the bag to show how superior he really was. First he did his usual "Goodbye Cornwall! Devon here we come!" routine as we crossed the Tamar, and for good measure turned and gave a friendly "Thank-you" bark to the car park attendant in Plymouth. His *pièce-de-résistance* he kept for Dingle's itself. Going up in the lift we said that we would go to the second floor to get some tools. "First floor—ladies' underwear!" intoned the lift attendant. Many got out but Toby did not budge. "Second floor—do-it-yourself!" and out marched Toby ahead of us and everyone else. We were as impressed as Zena and immensely proud.

I bought a lovely Japanese hatchet and hammer, an electric frypan (generator, here we come!) lots of kitchen gadgets and finished up buying a Peter Scott wildfowl record. I also browsed through language records trying to decide which new language I would study in my spare time. After all, an island on the south-western outposts of our shores was as likely a place as any for the landing of foreign spies or other aliens up to some nefarious business or other. Not being able to make up my mind which country presented the greatest danger I decided that I would make do with the French and German, and brush up my knowledge of these. We then went on to the cash-and-carry and loaded up the car with enough tinned and dried food to last us until the next Ice Age joined us to the mainland again.

The rest of the week was predictably unpredictable. We expected callers, of course. Word had got around, we supposed, that we were about to move over and so the regulars turned up with offers of help. Mr and Mrs Whitehouse, still very concerned on our behalf, volunteered to come with us on Saturday to show us how to start the generator. The rest of the country was still ice-bound and as it was early February bad weather and gales were not only possible, but, as we now know, extremely likely. The worst storms we have had on the island, with many disasters out at sea in the area, have been during February. We did not think that Mr Whitehouse in his serious state of health should commit himself, for having promised we knew that that kind gentleman would hate to back out on his word. Instead we agreed that he should explain how the generator worked. I found it to be quite beyond me but Babs seemed to follow what he was talking about to some extent. I tried to look intelligent so that he would not be too worried about us but I was banking on Babs' superior mechanical ability, to which she in fact makes little claim, to get the thing going. We told them about the foaming brown liquid that gushed malodorously out of the tap. Mr Whitehouse said that a weed must have got into the water storage tank in the wood. How right he was! When later we found the tank it looked as though "Doomwatch" had been on location there. Great leering fronds of a particularly malevolent species of weed festooned the nearby trees and draped themselves menacingly round the tank as if in the act of throttling it. I swear that baleful eyes leered at us as the tentacles embraced and penetrated into our precious water store inch by inch even as we watched.

"Sodium chlorate is what you want," said Mr Whitehouse, and sodium chlorate was added to our still growing list.

There were at least twenty-five callers that day, although some of them did not really count as they were the same ones calling again and again, like Ruth, Zena, Peter, Wren, Duncan, "Pipes-over-the-water", Ruth's mother and father and Mr Nancollas (now highly delighted that he could at last have his own store back). In addition the reps with whom we had become acquainted at the catering exhibition now began to call. One nice touch was when we were able to offer the Twinings' tea rep a cup of his own free sample. As they all called we ordered vast quantities of detergent, coffee, dried milk, Horlicks and drinking chocolate, which was a little optimistic considering the state of our water supply. Then there were the appointments with insurance agents.

If insurance had seemed complicated before, the intricacies of trying to cover our far flung little empire of house, cottages, farm buildings, boats, engines and boathouse as well as all the contents and equipment, for storm damage as well as the usual cover, almost defeated us. We were insistent that everything, but everything, should be covered for storm damage whatever the cost, for we had experienced enough of the force of the elements to realise what havoc they can wreak. Consequently our premiums were extremely high. "Never mind," we thought "come wind or high water, we are covered." How naïve can one be. We found to our cost that we had not been astute enough and we now know that money cannot buy everything. It may not buy love or health and we would add to that that it cannot buy insurance. When last year we lost the boathouse and its entire contents, three outboard engines, an inboard engine, three boats, a thirty-foot barge, farm equipment and two very good mowers we put in a very modest claim for £1000. Our claim was settled for £120 and not a penny more could we get. The inboard engine alone had cost £140, and our premiums over the last few years would have bought us a couple of fine boats with engines to spare. When a year or so ago a landslide demolished the pumphouse for our spring water supply in the cliff that was rated as an "act of God" with nil compensation and it was only due to the courtesy of the assessor, and a tree that had conveniently fallen in with the rest of the debris that it was pronounced that God was only 75 per cent to blame and we were awarded 25 per cent of our claim, which at least was enough to pay an engineer to estimate for a new one. We are of the opinion that most of the disasters of that nature here should not be blamed on God. To us that is sheer blasphemy, for they are nothing less than acts of the Devil, and that proviso not being mentioned in insurance policies, I reckon we should get our full whack, just like anyone else on the mainland, but maybe they do not get it either. Perhaps the next best thing to owning an island is to own your very own insurance firm. I must be fair, though. I had another letter from my photographic firm—the same day that the twenty-five visitors called—to say that the Pentax could be repaired after all. This was at considerable expense to the insurers, for the camera was almost a complete write-off, and six months later I received it in good working order without a penny cost to myself.

Babs and I did not see much of each other during what we hoped would be the last week we should be officially domiciled on the mainland. She of course was fully occupied during the day at school and now, as is usual with teachers, but not always acknowledged by the general public, after school activities were encroaching on her private life. Over the years I have seen this done with enthusiasm and dedication and it should be recognized by those who only remark about the long school holidays.

One of Babs' activities at that time was to sit on a brains trust at the local youth club. As usual, she was more concerned with her appearance than with her intellect. Not having much claim to either during this period I was not invited but I had a couple of problems of my own. The first was a visit to the dentist. I had had toothache the week before and Ruth had kindly let me have her appointment. Mr Leck had said that the tooth would have to come out and the next day was the day fixed for this. I was not looking forward to the visit—not that one ever does—but the reason I was less enthusiastic than usual was that the knee that had been injured on Sunday was troubling me. I could not sleep at night for the pain was like neuralgia, also the leg from the instep to above the knee was very swollen and a nasty black/blue colour. It was painful to walk on, and I felt quite sorry for myself when I turned up at the dentist's surgery. To my great relief Mr Leck said that the tooth would not have to come out after all and a stopping would do. He added however that a wisdom tooth would have to be extracted at my next appointment. This I thought I could not afford to lose as I had always been short on wisdom teeth, the full quota never arriving in the first place. I reckoned I would need all the aids to wisdom I could lay on to keep us on the paths of sanity, but Mr Leck no doubt thought that day was long past. Who in their right minds, with a full set of wisdom teeth in working order would embark on the venture we had undertaken, off the wild Cornish coast in mid-winter of all times? As the future was to prove, there was no end to the possibilities of madness that one could get up to, for there is something about island life that breeds ideas like the yeast in fermenting wine.

Back at the cottage Duncan called on his way to the doctor. He apparently had suffered no bad effects from his accident with the tractor and we hoped that the visit to the doctor had nothing to do with this. On the spur of the moment I decided to go with him and have my knee looked at.

Usually one assumes that if there is not a broken limb most minor injuries cure themselves, given time, but I was going to need my leg on that island, and not only was it not so far curing itself, but it seemed to be getting worse, and was beginning to look like an elephant's leg. Dr Harvey said that he did not think that it was phlebitis. Good God! the thought had never entered my head, and I am not often lagging behind in the imagination stakes. Apparently a deep vein had been damaged and had flooded the leg and I would have to wear an elastic bandage for at least three weeks. It would be very painful for those three weeks he said and gave me some painkillers. He also informed me that he would be unable to travel to the island to look after me. I did not know if this meant that there was no Health Service on the island or whether he himself could not come and it would have to be someone else if the necessity arose. If the former surely I would not have to pay the full amount of the National Health stamp—happy thought—until I remembered what happened the last time I had official dealings over this all-important scrap of paper, and I certainly did not want to land myself with a job in Looe or I should never get to live on the island. I dismissed the problem, to be sorted out in the future, for there was enough to occupy us in setting ourselves up on our dream island, although in attaining it was often more like a nightmare.

The two cottages presented a bit of a problem. If we did not do something about them they would soon become derelict. The Smuggler's cottage, which had not been lived in since the Whitehouse's gardener left the previous summer, was growing black fungi over the ceiling and inside walls, and the lovely enclosed walled garden in which grew peaches and figs as well as apples, pears, plums, blackcurrant and masses of roses, had become completely overgrown in those few short months; the absence of frost allowing the tangled undergrowth to burgeon all year through. The other cottage of which the one-time converted barn was part, had apparently been used partly as a packing station for the daffodils. Already floorboards were rotted and stove in as you trod on them and one's feet went through to the earth beneath. We did not relish the idea of seeing them become complete ruins. The only choice, apart from doing a Queen Elizabeth I act and doing the rounds of sleeping in each place in turn was, we thought, to put them in good order and accommodate friends when they came to help. The O'Neills and Peter Steele and his family from the art school were bringing their tents to camp that first year to help us pioneer but it would be something to aim for if we could house a future generation of helpers in the cottages. Thus were sown some more seeds of conservation. We were in fact a little ahead of this trend as far as the general population was concerned, for at that time the word "conservation", if it were bandied around in ordinary social circles, meant little more than the underlying principle of one major political party, or a constipated condition of mind attributed to it if you happened to belong to the other.

As a start in this direction we decided to acquire some bits of furniture for the cottages, and went along to Oliver Hicks' fortnightly sale which was conveniently due that week. Mr Hicks was—as the reader may remember—the estate agent in East Looe from whom we had bought our two little cottages in Bassett Court at what now seemed a lifetime ago. It was therefore with a feeling of nostalgia that Babs and I went along to the preview. These auction sales are really a part of the local social life, and Mr Hicks and Mr Nancollas take it turn and turn about to hold them in East and West Looe respectively. We both felt rather guilty as we passed Nancollas's store on West Looe Quay on our way to cross the bridge to East Looe for we knew that we had put the spanner in the works, however unintentionally, as far as Mr Nancollas and West Looe auctions were concerned. As we could not attend the sale itself we left a bid for two iron bedsteads and a wall cupboard. The next evening we called in and found that we had acquired all three items—12/6d each for the bedsteads and 10/– for the cupboard, which with the commission came to £1.18.0. Oh! happy days of pre-decimalisation and raging inflation. We loaded them on the car and for the rest of the week, which included an invitation to visit a lady potter, they went with us wherever we went, for we felt that it would have been adding insult to injury to put them in Nancollas's store. We must have looked like refugees searching for a home, which in a way was what we were.

It was becoming imperative that we make our final move soon and hoped that the following Saturday would be "D" Day for the longer we stayed on the mainland the greater the amount of our acquisitions grew. Every time I went on a foray for kitchen equipment and foodstores it became a compulsion to pick up some more seeds, fertiliser and a book or books. Wren now told us that we needed cement and Ruth said that a couple of tiler's hammers were essential. Not, as one might suspect, that we were going to take up tiling in our spare time, useful as this skill would have been, for it is almost routine that tiles fly off the roofs every winter, but because Ruth's father advised us that we should need them for cultivating on a hillside. His holding at Shutta was on a steep hillside and in this aspect the island is similar. All the daffodil fields slope down from the top of the island and there is only one spot that is a plateau of sorts and this is the lawn at the back of the house. Even this looks man-made for on two sides it finishes abruptly on high banks buttressed by dry stone walls. This is a fine flat lawn that Mr Whitehouse used as a croquet lawn; we doubted whether we would have the time for keeping it in such fine condition or for playing croquet.

It was nevertheless quite incredible what we thought we should have time for, and the more we dreamed about our future island life the more our minds tumbled with ideas. We now had enough stores and kitchen equipment to start a large scale catering establishment, although our collection was intended as a hedge against total isolation from civilisation and after our experiences in trying to set foot on the island this seemed a distinct possibility. We had amassed sufficient seeds, seed potatoes, fertilisers and sacks of sphagnum peat to run a market garden extending over the whole twenty-two-and-a-half acres, although only five were under cultivation and these given over mostly to the daffodils. The photographic equipment and impedimenta would have made a studio photographer green with envy; the stock of film was enough to take a shot every minute of every daylight hour for months to come, or so it looked. In addition I had acquired materials for colour processing to add to the other darkroom work. The collection of stones that we had made over the years went over by the sack load together with Babs' rather splendid and professional stone cutting and polishing machine for this was before lapidary became the popular hobby it is today and the many types of small polishing machines now obtainable were not yet generally on the market. The pottery equipment and sacks of clay and glazes were to be housed in a building large enough to serve as a pottery for a whole art school.

We now added tins of paint against the time when we could decorate the two cottages, plus plenty of timber and nails for repairs—the electric drill and attachments would certainly come in useful for this, always supposing we had electricity. The printing press would take care of any ambitions we had in that line, and the woodcarving tools would soon turn driftwood into masterpieces. We had stacks of canvases, oil paints, pastels, sketch books and the rest of the paraphernalia of painting to stun the art world with our creations. In fact, with my penchant of putting last things first I had brought some rather good beading to frame these masterpieces although so far we had scarcely put brush to canvas. We had of course the equipment for other crafts to fill in our spare time, metalwork, lino cuts, collage, marquetry, copper enamelling, to name but a few. Although Babs now realised that apart from school holidays she would be lucky to get to the island at week-ends except in the summer months, she was not daunted by her huge collection of semi-precious stones, but in fact surveyed it with relish.

For leisure we had our books and music. Our collection of musical instruments was quite considerable, and was to be crowned in the future with the church organ, while for listening we had the stereo tape recorder and record player. Our growing library would extend our knowledge of marine life, ornithology, geology, archaeology, small boats, astronomy, and fishing. As Wren succintly remarked, it would take two hundred years to read all the books we were taking with us. If between any of these activities we got tired at looking at stars through the telescope we could always make a few bricks with the brick-making machine. It might be a good time to say now that the future, hazardous, unpredictable and frustrating as it often became, did not and does not take the edge off our enthusiasm; on the contrary, it sparks off even more ideas. To change the metaphor we have found that after a winter of minor and sometimes major catastrophies, when our ardour seems temporarily to fade, the spring comes without fail, the sap begins to rise, and new ideas and projects flower and flourish again.

The fact that we were going to live on this lonely island had an extraordinary effect on people. An older generation than ours thought that we were completely demented; our contemporaries were divided into those who wished they had the courage to join us, and the others, the majority, who blanched with fear at the thought. Those who were solidly behind us and who yearned to come too were not only those who were half our age, but an even younger generation going down to the five—to nine-year-olds. With sparkling eyes they helped us with their might and main, and now as teenagers say that it was the most exciting time of their lives, and one they will never forget.

With all the enterprises with which we were engaged we were, I am sure the reader will agree, not exactly the doddering type. Hard physical effort was required just to land our goods on the island. Once there, one had to be extremely fit and resilient to endure the sustained arduous exertions required to live there. We both frequently have been waist deep in raging surf trying to stop the weighty *Islander* from going broadside on. We have had to hack our way through fallen trees, sawing off huge branches that have blocked our main and only path after winter storms and once when I was alone on the island twenty one hundredweight sacks of coal had perforce to be slung overboard on to the beach below high water mark as it was too dangerous to beach the *Islander*. I had no choice, if they were not to be swept out with the next tide, but to move each one up over the banking shingle and seaweed and up to the house. So many of the conditions with which we have to contend could not be coped with by anyone of advanced years nor viewed with equanimity even by those of middle age. You can imagine our utter astonishment therefore when some little time after we had gone to live on the island some visitors landed and said. "We hear that two old ladies own the island." "If so, I am one of them," I replied tartly. I must add, though, that their amazement was even greater than ours, for they could not believe that we were the ladies in question.

Apart from all these occupations we had in mind that in our spare time we would write a history of the island. The clerk to the council had kindly allowed us to sit in the council chamber and take notes from their original copy of *Bond's History of Looe*, published in 1823, which referred to even earlier histories. As a recent purchaser of *Encyclopaedia Britannica* I was the proud possessor of a sheet of tokens, each one of which entitled one to a specialised research on any chosen subject. One of these tokens I had duly sent off with a request for a detailed research into the early history of the island. We hoped that this when it came, together with our notes, would · form the basis of our own book.

Tales of smuggling, buried treasure and tunnels to the mainland we had of course heard many times and we hoped that by our own research and checking facts locally, interesting details would come to light about this colourful period of the island's history.

The island is rich, too; in legend; the most fascinating being that Joseph of Arimathea was said to have landed here with the Child Christ on his way to Glastonbury. The fact that the chapel, dating back to 1139 at least, came under the see of Glastonbury when Benedictine monks were on the island had given rise to much speculation to others before us and we were surprised that there was no record of an excavation ever having been made of the chapel site. The possibility therefore of having one was well to the forefront of our future plans.

To add to the folklore of the island it is said to be haunted and there are accounts of ghosts being sighted, but like many hauntings they cannot be authenticated. When we came to live on the island we certainly felt that a very strong influence existed which others apart from ourselves claimed to have felt. This influence has a way of inspiring some artistic people so that they are able to produce of their very best. Others feel as soon as they set foot on the island that they must help in some way. It is almost a compulsion with them as they slave away for the whole of their holiday, not satisfied unless in some small way at least they are able to leave their mark. Wherever their journeyings take them later they treasure the memories, even years after, and from all parts of the world we hear from them: Life for them will never be quite the same again, for they have been touched with island magic. One visitor, Duncan Chapman, brings plants from Africa, South America, California or from whatever country he has been visiting, and plants them on the island during his few hours stay. Other dedicated enthusiasts make their annual homage and during their stay will make or do things which will be of practical use; they will build walls, extend the jetty, make seats, plumb in water, erect water tanks, clear tracks, till the land, sow, weed, cut the fields and decorate the cottages. Not only will they pay for their holiday but after they have gone away they will send presents and cheques. Among these are the young, about whom so much criticism is made, and whom we have found to be some of the island's most ardent devotees. Even casual visitors will give more than is asked for the crafts, and only the other day someone insisted on paying £2 for a cup of tea! So if you should hear an argument going on in the cafe/craft shop you can almost be sure that it is someone insisting on paying over the odds.

It must be said that all this helps us to keep the island unspoilt and uncommercialised for in aiming at this as our ideal, it is run at a loss and we have to subsidise the project from our own income. Nevertheless it is a strange phenomenon that people should have this attitude in these days of strikes, protest marches, and student and customer revolt. On the other hand the island has a way of rejecting those of whom it disapproves; in these unfortunate visitors it seems to bring out an almost evil streak. We can spot them as soon as they set foot on the island. Within a few minutes of their arrival we know that before their time is up they will be hot foot back to the mainland, with its supermarkets, bingo halls and pubs just as soon as a boat can carry them. It is not that they are necessarily city or urban conditioned, for we have many townsfolk who have become islanders but instinctively we know that the island is going to reject them. They will shoot back faster than they came, denied the touch of island magic. We cannot wait for the moment of their going, for they have a disturbing influence on all who reside here. We cannot explain this, we can only record that it happens. Happily they are in the minority and leave us to wonder about the almost magnetic power of the island.

Chapter 11
End of dress rehearsal and first night

On Friday, 12th February at midnight we loaded up the *Orlando* with the last remnants of our possessions from Nancollas's store, plus all our recent acquisitions including the chlorate of lime to purify the water tank. This we would have to clear ourselves if we wished to have drinkable water. We were a little surprised about this, for one of the legacies we had acquired with the island was a final demand for the rates. We had paid this without giving it too much thought, but it now began to dawn on us, and currently with the tremendous increase in rates, with growing concern, that no public services are provided for the island at all, but regular as clockwork in come the demand for rates. At this particular time our only real concern was whether chlorate of lime would be any more palatable than weed-infested water, but trustingly we heaved it on board. We had had a busy evening with everyone milling round the cottage, charging in and out like Charing Cross station in the rush hour—so much so that we actually had our evening meal standing up behind the counter of the kitchen and dispensing coffee to the very last dregs of our mainland supply. We finally got to bed at 2.45 a.m. and by then the wind was already freshening from the north-west, a direction that in winter can mean sudden violent squalls accompanied by slashing rain. Luckily we were not aware of this possibility and slept soundly, for on the morrow with any luck we should be resting our heads on our desert island.

"Take off" was planned for 8.30 a.m. It was a sunny gusty morning and the weather forecast for our area was "snow, ice, gales and storms." In spite of this Wren thought that it would be all right to go. Opinion was divided about this and by the time "let's go" had won the day it was 9.30 a.m. and the tide was receding fast. Earlier Wren had taken the *Orlando* out into Looe Bay beyond the harbour. As we had loaded her up the night before all we had to do was to ferry ourselves out to her in the metal boat. The outboard refused to start up so we had to row out. Two trips and we were all aboard the *Orlando*—Wren, Babs, Ruth and myself and Peter, who was coming to see if there was any way we could run the deep freeze from the generator, always supposing we could work it at all (at present it only ran for a part of each day when required and not at all during the hours of sleep). Toby, Charles and a few last minute stores and clothes were to be towed behind the *Orlando* in the metal boat.

It was dead calm in the bay as we were sheltered from the offshore north-west winds by Hannafore and the westerly rocks exposed by the fast receding tide. Once we were out of the shelter of this arm of the shore the sea began to cut up and was very choppy indeed. Soon we ran into squalls which drenched poor Charles and Toby with sheets of spray. We were to moor in the Jetty Bay and ferry in by the metal boat. Unfortunately there was no shelter in the bay from the north-west squalls, which became even more frequent and violent. Very gingerly Babs, Ruth and I lowered ourselves into the metal boat to join Toby while Wren and Charles changed places so that Wren could row us ashore.

Though not quite as bad as the time when I had to jump for it as from an express train and clung suspended from the jetty posts, the landing was hazardous enough. Wren decided that the beach in the bay was the best bet and between squalls he rowed us through a narrow channel between the rocks, and we were more or less shot ashore on to mounds of seaweed as though we had been slung out of a catapult. While Wren rowed back to fetch Peter and Charles we slowly and carefully made our way, sinking in seaweed up to our knees and clambering over slippery rocks until at last we climbed the slope up the cliff above the jetty. It took several of these journeys to get everything up and on to the house. By then a good three quarters of an hour had elapsed and we fully expected that the other three would be ashore by the time we had made our last trip.

There was no sign of them, and looking out to the *Orlando* we could see no sign of life at all; no Wren, no Peter, no Charles. In fact we had the eerie feeling that we were gazing on another *Marie Celeste*. We waited perhaps another half an hour, and during this time our imaginations ran riot as we listened to the screaming of the wind as it tore across from the north-west whipping up the sea into a broiling mass of foam, and topped by the wailing of the gulls as they rode the wind. We had a feeling of impending doom and it was with a gasp of relief that we saw Wren clamber over the side of the *Orlando*, albeit alone, and row ashore to us. Peter, who had not been keen that we should come in the first place because of the weather, apparently liked the look of it even less when we ran into the squalls. Now that it was worsening every minute he did not fancy landing and not being able to return to the mainland, so he wanted to return at once. Wren, having told us all this, recommended that we too return immediately as he did not like the look of the weather either.

Instead, we mutinied. Hitherto we had done everything at Wren's bidding. Unquestioningly, through storms, before the break of dawn, in the pitch dark of a bitter winter's night, swamped, frozen, pitched around by the elements, all but tossed overboard, we had obeyed orders without complaint. But to be told to return tamely to the mainland now, that we would not do. With herculean efforts we had at last set foot to stay on our island; we were equipped, prepared and feverishly eager to rest our heads there for the very first time after months of waiting and many weeks of endeavour. Now, with the magic moment within our grasp, it was to be snatched away. We could not take it and suddenly we blew out tops. "Nothing", we said firmly, "would induce us to return to the mainland. We were here and here we meant to stay—and that was that." Wren very reluctantly agreed. This reluctance we realised later was not due to the weather conditions, but to the fact that he was disinclined to leave us there while he had to go back to the mainland with the others and be separated from the island project on which he was so keen. For some reason he said that we must keep the metal boat with us. Whether he thought we might change our minds and want to row back to the mainland we did not enquire, but we would have agreed to anything so long as he did not try to persuade us to return with him. Ruth, he said, was to come out to the *Orlando* so that he could get back on board, and then she was to row herself round to the main beach.

We watched the *Orlando* sail away, and I then went down the path to the main beach to help Ruth beach the metal boat. The reason it could not be brought in to the jetty beach, which was nearer to where the *Orlando* had been moored, was that the winter spring tides crashed right up on to the cliffs there at high tide, and would have smashed to bits any boat left there. The main beach was a wide sloping expanse of shingle and sand and was reckoned to be a safe haven for boats to be tied up. An enormous barge was kept there as well as a winch and the boathouse. From photographs it would appear that this last had been there for about a hundred years and we never believed for one moment that these could be swept away. For some years, summer and winter, we were able to keep two boats tied up to the trees well above high water mark. This, then, was where Ruth was to bring in the metal boat. Unfortunately with the wind being directly on-shore there, it was exposed to the full force of the squalls which had grown in intensity. I arrived to find Ruth up to her waist in surf trying to hold on to the boat which was being swept broadside on in the breakers. It looked in imminent danger of capsizing and submerging Ruth or carrying her out to sea in the long vicious runs. Luckily Babs arrived on the scene and sending Ruth up to the house to change into dry clothing, Babs and I, à la Wren, tried to lever the heavy boat ashore with the use of planks which were stacked up by the boathouse. We extended the cable of the winch to its limit and slowly, inch by inch, levered the boat up to within a rope's length of the cable end. It was a difficult operation, for all the time the surf was dragging at the boat and pulling our feet from under us. At last we managed to attach the rope to the cable but twice the rope broke and twice the boat was sucked back into the breakers. Babs hung on for dear life to the stern, and as I was the one with the rope I tried frantically to tie a knot to join the broken ends. Now it will have been apparent that the intricacies of knot tying had always defeated me. Years ago I had dismissed it into the limbo of life's failures together with sewing, making custard and learning Latin. Suddenly there was no choice, for Babs could not leave her end of the boat or it would have been swept out to sea. Desperation is a good teacher. Belaying the rope around my middle to keep the bows of the boat steady and to give myself a bit of spare rope that was not dragged taut with every surge of the sea I attempted to join the broken ends. The resulting knot will not be found in any naval, boy scout or girl guide manual, but Glory Be! it held. With spray more or less coming out of my ears I christened it a Great Granny knot and many times it has saved the day in similar desperate situations. The only difference being that it is never quite the same knot twice; on the other hand would it not be a very peculiar world indeed if all great grandmothers were identical?

A few more heaves of the planks and we were clear of the breakers. The boat was full of water and too heavy to tilt over to empty, but after much bailing out we were able to winch her up high and dry above the tide line.

After we too had changed into dry clothing we decided that as we were all quite exhausted by this time we would take it in turns to have a rest, one of us being left on watch. Memory does not provide the reasoning behind this but presumably it was so that someone would be able to give the alarm if the island should take off in the storm force winds and churning seas. Toby seemed very happy. He had settled in as though he had lived on islands all his life and was the only one who opted not to rest.

We managed to find some driftwood and got a fire going in the lounge—the kitchen still being an impenetrable forest of tea chests. We had bought a certain amount of fresh water with us but finding a tank of rainwater outside the house we boiled some of that over the fire and made ourselves one of the most welcome cups of tea we had ever had, while we reviewed the situation. By now the light was fading fast and we decided that the first priority was to get the generator going, not so much for lighting because so far we had not unearthed our supply of electric light bulbs, but because we were most anxious to use the record player and play *Bali Hi* from *South Pacific*, as we thought that this would be the most appropriate music to play on our first night aboard our island.

It was dark by the time we reached the generator room which was at the end of the path, not far from the main beach. By the light of a torch we peered at intricate diagrams on a large instruction sheet. According to this the generator was a Lister *Start-o-Matic* and would start up automatically with the flick of any electric light switch on the island. It was soon apparent that it was not going to do it this way tonight, or, as we subsequently found out, any other night for a long time. Although we did not realise it then, the batteries which provided the power for this automatic starting were completely dead through not being used for so many months, and the electrical box controlling this was out of action for the same reason and also because of the penetration of the damp sea atmosphere. It was all quite Greek to us but Babs, as the car driver, read out and interpreted the instructions, and gave us her version of what she thought they meant. One thing was obvious; the thing would have to be started manually. This meant swinging a handle and simultaneously moving little lever-like things and pushing them into specified points. Ruth was detailed for some bits of this mechanical dexterity. Babs, with torch in mouth, conducted from the "score" at the same time pulling and pushing levers that had rusted up from lack of use, a feat a contortionist would have found difficult. This left me as the swinger. Now I am no swinger, neither by inclination nor physique. I grant you I was brought up on eurhythmics, could swing a cricket bat and other weapons in the gameswomanship artillery tolerably well, but muscle hardly came into it. In fact the reverse was the case, rhythm taking the place of strength. In any case cricket bats, tennis, badminton and squash racquets and hockey sticks are inanimate objects; they have no life of their own and only generate the power you give them.

When it comes to objects that leap into life the moment you touch them I am just plain lily-livered.

An instance of this happened, I am ashamed to admit, during the war. While we were awaiting the time when we could volunteer for the W.R.N.S. or what have you, some of us filled in our spare time by joining a few auxiliary bodies such as part time Land Army, Home Guard and the Fire Brigade of the factory where our London Offices had been evacuated. The Fire Brigade consisted of teams of four, each of which took it in turns to guard the factory at night against attack by incendiary bombs. This was a distinct possibility as we were still near enough to London to see the glare of the red sky as London burned under the incessant attacks. The main piece of equipment was a trailer pump and a fire hose pipe, and our Fire Chief instructed us in the use of the pump, had us climbing up thirty-foot ladders with hose pipe over shoulder on to roofs, got us crawling under canopies of smoke so that we could instruct others, made us practise the fireman's lift and generally train us in how to deal with the various hazards with which we might have to cope. On fire duty nights we would get up our own alarm drills, screeching on the whistle and racing up the fire escape of the deserted factory building at dead of night with hose pipe over shoulder trying to beat the record each time. All this was exciting and thoroughly enjoyable, but there was one aspect of it at which I quivered with fright. This was starting up the engine of the trailer pump which meant swinging a handle, as on a car. As captain of my team responsible for calling these practices I could hardly opt out of starting up the engine on account that I was afraid. It would have been disastrous for morale and, I told myself, just the sort of loophole that Hitler would have been looking for, so I just had to grit my teeth, shut my eyes, and swing. I considered that that little operation was my major war effort and deserved an award for bravery. Along with the certificate on behalf of the King for services with "Dad's Army" and the one from My Lords of the Admiralty for the privilege of serving in the W.R.N.S. should be a medal specially inscribed to me, who "With great courage while under stress and strain, without regard to wild fears, did swing the handle of the trailer pump under her command." Maybe others feel the same way about this starting handle business; or maybe I was frightened by a clockwork toy when I was a baby; only a psychiatrist would know.

The fact remained that I was faced with this problem all over again, only this was no starting handle of a car; it was a massive affair, and looked as though it was capable of starting up the Queen Mary all by itself. According to Babs voice in the darkness you had to turn it rapidly until you got compression, "or convulsions" I thought grimly as she considerately shone the torch for me. I could not even turn it round, let alone rapidly. "You have to push it right in first," said Ruth. "Look, like this." She pushed the handle in and swung it round in no time at all, then went back to her post waiting for me to swing so that she could push in the vital bits. "It's a knack," she added. "You are right there," I thought bitterly, "you also need the arm of an all-in wrestler." Desperation again came to my aid. I swung and swung until I thought my arm would come out of its socket. Suddenly I felt resistance. Although I did not know it, I had "got compression". "Swing harder!" they both yelled pushing things in like mad. Babs shouted that I was to push in a twiddly bit too—she had just read it. Suddenly the generator roared into life and a light slowly came on, as in an Agatha Christie thriller. It was like some fiendish magic. Open-mouthed I gazed in wonder and then in horror, for in the excitement of success I had left the handle in—well no one had told me to take it out—and there it was, spinning madly round and round. "Good God! it will take off like when those Scotsmen throw the hammer" I thought frantically. I was in the direct line of fire—there was only one thing to do—hoof it-and at the double. I shot out of the door, and panic stricken, looked over my shoulder to see if it were following me; instead the light went out and the engine clanked into silence—the others had coolly turned the engine off.

We had another go. I got compression, we all pushed in our twiddly bits, the engine began to clank again, then throbbed rhythmically, the light slowly came on, and with great aplomb I pulled the handle out. Success at last! It was just as well for we had to go through this routine for another two months before the weather was fit enough for an engineer to come out and make it work automatically again.

Back at the house we found to our astonished delight that we had some electric light there too. We did not bother to find a bulb for the lounge for the driftwood fire gave a warm flickering glow, a fitting accompaniment to the roar of the sea below. We boiled up some more water for coffee and made omelettes over the fire. It seemed to us that no coffee had ever been so fragrant nor a meal more delectable. We found an electric point for the record player and happily tossed more logs on the fire as we listened to the haunting melody of "Bali Hi". Toby sat with us, very much at home and none the worse for his drenching of spray and rough crossing.

We Bought an Island

As the generator had been started manually it had to be stopped manually too, so down Babs and I went to the generator room and just by the touch of a switch stilled its mighty roar and plunged the island into darkness. This done we trudged, as we would for many nights to come, up the shingle path under the darkling woods beyond the Smugglers' cottage and so back to our house on the cliffs. Once there, with the help of a small oil lamp rather like Aladdin's lamp, we found some mattresses, cleared a space on the bare boards of the lounge floor, and just as we were, without getting undressed we all three and Toby lay side by side just like sausages in a pan. The full moon had broken through the scudding clouds sparkling on the wild sea below and bathing us in its soft light. As we lay there in front of the blazing driftwood fire a light flashed on the wall above the fireplace. It came and went at irregular intervals but in a rhythmic pattern and our contentment was complete when we realised that it was from Eddystone Lighthouse, 12½ miles away and our nearest neighbour.

So at last we had come to our heritage; the island that had dominated our thoughts for so long, and the realisation of a dream cherished since childhood.

As we rested there side by side we thought of the struggle, the uncertainties and the drama in achieving this momentous point in our lives. Now at last the months of endeavour had culminated in bringing us to this, the beginning of our new and uncharted life. For a long time feverish thoughts jostled each other, defeating sleep as we anticipated with eagerness the challenges before us. What would the future hold? The possibilities seemed limitless and infinitely enthralling.

At last sleep gently quietened our restless minds. As we drifted off towards tomorrow we felt we were on the brink of a great adventure, but if we could have forseen what lay ahead we would have been astonished to know that the hazardous events of the last few weeks were but the overture.

The curtain was about to rise on sufficient scenes of comedy, tragedy and drama to fill a book.